Sanctify the Soul

180 Days of Devotions & Poems to
Sanctify the Soul

Laura K Ford

For Diana

Additional Christmas and New Year's Devotions can be found in the back of this devotional starting on page 318.

Day 1
Sanctify the Soul

May God Himself, the God of peace, sanctify you through and through. 1 Thessalonians 5:23a

Lord, sanctify me wholly,
Leaving sin lost in the grave.
Where I long for only holy thoughts,
And my darkened past watch fade.

Lord, sanctify me wholly,
Yet not for self—sought fame,
But to feel the joy of cleansing,
Every moment of the day!

Lord, sanctify me wholly,
To be used beyond compare,
That I'd be a holy vessel,
And of Your Spirit, well aware!

Day 2
An Image Worth Reflecting

And I—in righteousness I will see Your face; when I awake, I will be satisfied with seeing Your likeness. Psalm 17:15

Imperfections glaring back,
All these insecurities!
Reminded what I have or lack,
This self—absorption's draining me!

A reflection of an earthly shell,
Though there must be more inside?
And, oh, that He would break my will,
Then His Spirit no longer I'd hide!

So instead of hearing all the lies,
And believing every one,
No matter how the enemy tries,
My Maker with me is not done!

For the truth of the matter is...

I am the image of perfection,
The image of the One,
A righteous, royal reflection,
Of God's One and Only Son!

Day 3
Sanctuary of God

When I tried to understand all this, it was oppressive to me till I entered the sanctuary of God... Psalm 73:16-17a

Challenging circumstances overwhelm us, making us feel isolated and abandoned. Even our physical body can be burdened in ways we thought were not possible. We may sit down to spend some quiet time with the Lord and not be able to put into words our current perplexity. Our need for clarity is so great that we may not even be able to pray. But as we begin to pour over God's Word, we feel the presence of the Holy Spirit and in an instant our mind is clear, our hearts are softened, and our souls revived. Prior to this, perhaps we tried to understand things that need not be understood, only surrendered and placed on the altar in the sanctuary of God. Once placed, our hearts are then able to bring forth praise! And thus forgetting our sorrow, we are able to bask in His glorious presence!

How lovely is Your dwelling place, O LORD Almighty. My soul yearns, even faints for the courts of the LORD; My heart and flesh cry out for the Living God. Psalm 84:1-2

You are awesome, O God, in Your sanctuary; the God of Israel gives power and strength to His people. Praise be to God! Splendor and majesty are before Him; strength and glory are in His sanctuary. Lift up

your hands in the sanctuary and praise the LORD.
Psalm 68:35, 96:6, 134:2

Awesome in Your Sanctuary!
See Him stand above the crowd.
All saints before Thee, bended knee,
With heads so humbly bowed.

Glorious in Your Sanctuary!
See splendor and majesty shine!
Strength and glory inhabit here,
Even creatures guard the Divine!

Reigning in Your Sanctuary!
See the carnelian, jasper hue!
Lamps ablaze, elders crowned,
They give Him the honor He's due!

Merciful in Your Sanctuary!
See the Lamb sacrificed and slain!
This crimson blood purchasing all debt,
Flowed from Emmanuel's veins!

Beautiful in Your Sanctuary!
No words can ever describe!
Both now and forever—Jesus our King,
Ascribe to the Lord, ascribe!

Day 4
The Promise Maker

"My eyes fail looking for Your promise..." You know with all your heart and soul that not one of all the good promises the Lord your God gave you has failed. Every promise has been fulfilled; not one has failed. Psalm 119:82a, Joshua 23:14

Abraham, a friend of God, never saw the promise of his descendants outnumbering the stars. Moses, the most humble man that ever lived, never stepped foot in the Promise Land. David, a man after God's own heart, never worshiped in the temple built by his son Solomon. John the Baptist, a man great in the sight of the Lord, never saw Christ being raised from the dead. If these men had only looked for God's promise, their eyes would have failed them. However, something they believed with all their heart and soul was that the promises of God are always fulfilled. If we only focus on the promise, we will never fully see the Promise Maker. Yes, His promises are great, but our Sovereign Lord is greater and oh so worthy of our patience. It may be that God is fashioning a description of your character right now as you wait on the promise He has made to you. Believe it with all your heart and soul, then move on— you have a Savior to seek!

But my eyes are fixed on You, Sovereign LORD; in You I take refuge..." Psalm 141:8

O LORD Almighty, blessed is the one who trusts in You. Psalm 85:12

Lord, help me to trust You even more,
My flesh is so frail, so weak.
Lord, help me to trust You even more,
For I don't feel I have the strength.

Lord, teach me to trust You even more,
My worries, they burden me.
Lord, teach me to trust You even more,
For temptations abound, indeed.

Lord, remind me to trust You even more,
My disappointments are frightening.
Lord, remind me to trust You even more,
For the past is still threatening.

Lord, break me in order to trust You more,
My heart sees this the only way.
Lord, break me in order to trust You more,
For when broken, close to You I stay.

Day 5
Freedom Found

*Now the Lord is the Spirit, and where the Spirit of the Lord is,
there is freedom. 2 Corinthians 3:17*

Sweet freedom, where you are, is where we want to
be!
The land our father's fought for, in truth and liberty!

A place we take for granted, a hope we toss aside.
Yet freedom was established through sacrifice and
nation's pride.

With limited perception, we gaze at other lands,
And with blinded introspection, we sit with folded
hands.

But for the one who's never had it, the one who'll
never be,
Freedoms only an objective, they and country never
see.

Yet to the one who is so desperate to live in such a
place,
Can be there in a moment, by God's mercy and His
grace.

Such a freedom is not temporal, you can't take it
away,
It is bound in realms eternal and there forever it will
stay!

And to the one who lives in freedom in a country of their own,
Do you still feel as a captive, although safe in your own home?

Then you must welcome the Spirit, to abide within your soul,
There to fill your life forever, with His truth to make you whole!

For where the Spirit of the Lord is, there is freedom for us all,
There is protection from the enemy, who seeks to make us fall.

There is eternal liberation from the chains that weigh us down,
Yes, where the Spirit of the Lord is, it is there freedom is found!

Day 6
The Flesh Fight

...for I am not practicing what I would like to do, but I am doing the very thing I hate. Romans 7:15b

Our greatest conflict, ninety-nine percent of the time, is with our own flesh. We can be our biggest disappointment. There are things about us that we wish we could change, wish we could overcome. I am not talking only of trials, I am talking about us, our habits, our nature, our quirks, our actions, our lack of self–discipline. Sadly, we might even look at this verse and think, "Well, even Paul struggled with doing things he did not want to do and not doing those things he wanted to do." Paul never meant for this verse to excuse our behavior. Within the context of the whole chapter in which we find this verse, Paul is presenting the flesh/spirit conflict, but not without giving us a way to conquer it. My husband often says,"Laura, there's no victory without a battle." Isn't that the truth! However, when it comes to our flesh, sometimes we refuse to even fight at all. We give in. We know there are things about us we want to change but we think fighting for that change isn't worth it. Or perhaps we look around at others with the same issues and we opt for joining the majority. Truth is, we don't like what we're doing and wish we could do something about it, but we don't. So we come to the same conclusion that Paul did, *Wretched man that I am* (Rom 7:24)! Unlike Paul, we tend to stop right there. However, he goes on and tells us that, we *do not walk according to the flesh but according to the Spirit* (Rom 8:4). We don't have to stay so wretched and continue to see ourselves or things about ourselves as disappointments. We can cry out to God to change us! We can beg Him not to let us continue to get away with our inconsistencies, with our lack of self-control, with whatever it is we wish we would just stop doing or start doing. With the power of the Holy Spirit, we can fight to be the people we were created to be in Christ!

What a disappointment,
All my inconsistencies,
I feel that I am wretched,
I am lost and in great need!

My convictions I've abandoned,
And I've let my morals slide.
Wishing to do what I'm commanded,
If I could to let go of my pride!

And I see this fight within me,
Within my heart, my soul, my mind,
It seems the flesh is overtaking me,
And winning every time!

Yet I declare, "You cannot have me!
You cannot control my mind!
There's a Spirit strong inside me,
Who walks a perfect line!"

This Spirit says, "Allow Him,
To fully have His way!"
And thus He takes over my being,
Praise the Lord, He's here to stay!

Day 7
Promise Keeper

Is not my house so with God? For He has made and everlasting covenant with me, ordered in all things and secured; for all my salvation and all my desire, will He not indeed make it grow? 2 Samuel 23:5, NASB

The rhetorical questions presented in Scripture about God often call us to recount His faithfulness. Just imagine King David, in his last song to his beloved Israel, furrowing his brow and saying in essence, "did He not and will He not?" *El*, the Mighty One, did He not prove Himself faithful to me in all my life? Did He not establish a lasting covenant with me? Did He not secure my lot and order my life according to His great love for me? And was it not for the completion of His salvation to me and all the desires He allowed my heart to long for? Will He not continue the work He started in my household? Will He not make it grow? If there is any doubt in our mind as to what God has done and is going to do in our lives, we need to remind ourselves, "did He not" and "will He not?" Did He not save me? Did He not extend His mercy to me time and time again? Will He not get me through this? Will He not continue to give me the desires of my heart? Will He not grow my household into a secure and loving place for me to continue the legacy He has given my children through Christ? Will He not deliver me from all my current trouble and stress? Apply that to whatever you are going through right this moment and then say, "oh, yes He did" and "oh, yes He will!" Sometimes we just need to get a little frustrated with ourselves for doubting the Mighty God we serve! There is not a promise He has made to us in His Word that we will not see perfectly fulfilled in Christ Jesus. Not one. He is a good Father to us!

Your goodness, Lord, is infinite,
Your kindness makes us whole,
Your mercies, never limited,
Your faithfulness from old!

Your provision on my household,
Your promise for our lives,
Your covenant unfolded,
Your precious blood, Your sacrifice!

Your call for us to love You,
Your command for us to trust,
Your promise You will come through,
Your Word, Lord, it's enough!

Day 8
Just Ask!

And God gave Solomon wisdom and understanding exceeding much, and largeness of heart, even as the sand that is on the sea shore. 1 Kings 4:29, KJV

Oh, if we would only ask! We know we ought to ask for wisdom, for insight, for discernment, but instead, we strive for a solution to fit our finite understanding. We do not trust that the wisdom from God is the ultimate answer to our restlessness. Infinite wisdom, given through the Holy Spirit, will release us from our limitations; release us from the pressure of trying to find elusive answers. Wisdom from God does not fit our perception of reality because it is supernatural. To receive this wisdom we must trust the Lord unashamedly. Ultimately our prayer ought to be, "Lord, give me the wisdom to know You, to have an understanding of Your Word that exceeds all bounds." If we could ask one thing, would we be like Solomon? Here was a man who desperately wanted to rule his people with God's wisdom, not his own. Do we care enough about others to ask for wisdom on how we ought to treat them, to pray for them, to interact with them? Perhaps we must be willing to have our heart stretched in such a way that it may very well burst wide open, making it completely exposed and vulnerable, in order for us to change. This is often a painful process but necessary for gaining the wisdom for understanding our needs and the needs of those around us. Every day we have the opportunity to ask and every moment God has the power to give. To His wisdom, there is no end.

If you then, though you are evil, know how to give good gifts to your children, how much more will your Father in heaven give the Holy Spirit to those who ask Him! Luke 11:13

Lord, I don't have because I don't ask,
I don't receive that which I don't grasp.
If I asked for grace, on me it would fall,
But instead I struggle and try to juggle it all.

If I asked for patience, I would experience peace,
But instead I'm restless, and over things, lose sleep.
If I asked for mercy, what a flood I'd possess,
But instead I dry up and forget I am blessed!

If I asked for provisions, I'd have all I need,
But instead I lack faith, forgetting the birds You feed.
If I asked for security, I'd with You always stand,
But instead I'm shaky, content wherever I land.

Lord, I don't have because I don't ask,
I don't receive that which I don't grasp.
But that doesn't mean I have to stay this way,
I want to ask for these things, and I'll start today!

Day 9
Within Our Power

Do not withhold good from those who deserve it, when it is in your power to act. Proverbs 3:27

There are so many people around us that are in tremendous need. Those needs vary from physical, to emotional, to spiritual needs. Although we may be aware of some of the problems, as to what depth they reach, we have no earthly idea. The trouble is, a lot of the time we do not make it our business to know. We assume. We assume that someone else will help and someone else will take the time to extend mercy. This is not for us to decide. Our openness and our love for others will be directly related to how we respond to their need when it is within our power to act. It is within our power to act more often than we realize or care to admit. God is always working in the lives of others in such complex and profound ways. If we are given the privilege to be an instrument of His workings in their lives, then we are the ones truly blessed. Do we trust the Lord enough to take care of us so that we are free to take care of others?

Let us give our prayers to those in distress,
While our worries and needs are laid to rest.
And we trust You to give us all we need,
So that our hands to give can be utterly freed!

Day 10
I Love You!

Love the Lord your God with all your heart and with all your soul and with all your strength. Deuteronomy 6:5

Oh Jesus, Yes! I love You!
More than life itself!
Your beauty takes my breath away,
I desire nothing else!

To have all of the wisdom,
The knowledge oft' pursued,
Still can't replace the ecstasy,
Of simply knowing You!

The peace, the love, the freedom,
Felt in Your loving arms,
Calms the knots within me,
Frees my soul from harm.

And no matter where You take me,
Since I know I must be trained,
Through quick and drastic measures,
My love for You, it shall remain!

For as much as I am broken,
The truth etched in my heart,
Will keep me safely hidden,
In Christ, never to part!

Day 11
The Longer Road

God did not lead them on the road through the Philistine country, though that was shorter... God lead the people around by the desert road toward the Red Sea... Exodus 13:17a &18 a

All throughout Scripture we are reminded of the Exodus, especially the miracle of the Red Sea when the waves parted and the Israelites crossed over on dry ground! However, details of the route to the Red Sea are not something we see again throughout the pages of Holy writ. That's because this part of the journey to the Red Sea paled in comparison to the miraculous crossing. Here we see that God did not lead them on the road that was shorter, instead *He lead the people around by the desert road*. It may be that God is leading you right now toward a miracle that will take place in your life, yet He has intended for you to take the long road to get there. You may even be able to see a shorter route and are quite perplexed as to why He will not allow you to take it. The shorter road may bring you closer to the miracle but not necessarily closer to the Lord. If God had allowed the Israelites to go the lesser distance, they may have encountered a battle they were not yet strong enough to fight, and in their weakness and fear, return to Egypt (Ex 13:17b). We may think that God has us go the distance because He wants to develop and strengthen our faith, and that may very well be true. However, He may also be protecting us from engaging in a battle that we are not ready to fight. We must trust the Lord to take us

down the path that is perfectly and presently suited
for us, however out of the way it may seem.

Father, why must I take this road?
So out of the way it seems?
Look! Lord, a shorter one,
Just down and across the ravine!
No, My child, this shorter road,
It is not the path for you.
You may have hoped it to be the way,
But it's not the path I choose.
Lord, don't you want me to save my strength,
And avoid a desert so dry?
Wouldn't you want me take a road,
That keeps me from asking why?
Sweet daughter, there is something,
That you simply cannot see.
And that something is a battle,
Raging in the Heavenlies.
If I were to send you down this short,
And seemingly steady road,
You would snap beneath the weight,
Of opposition un-foretold.
So do not worry if this journey,
Is taking a little bit longer,
For it is by this way that I will cause,
My miracle to grow stronger!

Day 12
Endure With Me

...I have had enough, Lord, he said. 1 Kings 19:4

Sometimes when we are at the point of saying, "Enough is enough, Lord," it usually means that we are so tired of the struggle that we really could care less what happens next. Things begin to lose their excitement and we are just tired— physically, mentally, and emotionally. Maybe we have been on such a high with God that once we come back down and face the reality of the dry, stifling desert of everyday life, we think that there is no way we can do the next thing. This is yet another time when our faith in God's sovereignty is crucial. Even though we have come, once again, to the end of ourselves, we have not come to the end of God Almighty. He has no end. There are still things He has for us to do, not just for ourselves, but for Him. It is in these times when we fully realize that our life does not belong to us, we are His servants. We keep going because He is not finished with us. God still has another journey for us to take, another mountain for us to climb. So get some rest and then let the Holy Spirit prepare your body, mind, and soul, for the next task at hand. He will supply you with *all* the strength you need.

Strengthened...he traveled forty days and forty nights until he reached Horeb, the mountain of God. 1 Kings 19:8

...being strengthened with all power according to His glorious might so that you may have great endurance and patience... Colossians 1:11

Endure with Me, the Spirit cries!
Open your soul and hide not your eyes.
How far will you go? Will you leave Me too?
Are you willing to do all I ask of you?
If you will only let Me, I will deepen your soul,
I will give you endurance, long-suffering from old.
Remember My power brought forth in the night,
A glorious strengthening, an astounding sight!
Three days of silence with the sting of death,
Long hours of questioning, doubt, and distress.
But what was I doing while souls despaired?
Wavering in unbelief, though by prophets prepared?
If only they had taken Me at My Word,
For the sight yet seen had surely been heard!
So when you can't fathom My plan for your life,
Do not succumb to vain toil or strife.
There's a depth to your soul which none can reach,
Lessons through suffering, only I can teach.
So please to not turn and from Me, run away,
For you will miss My Presence, unless you stay!
So suffer long My Beloved! The end is in sight!
I will turn mourning into dancing, give you songs in the night!
See there is no limit to what I can do,
If only you'll wait, I will deliver you soon!

Day 13
Proper Time

For there is a proper time and procedure for every matter, though a man's misery weighs on him heavily. Ecclesiastes 8:6

When we are under tremendous stress and anxiety, there is a tendency to do things in haste. Under certain strenuous circumstances it is also very difficult to discern the best course of action in *any* given matter. It's times like these when our dependency on the Holy Spirit's counsel is crucial. The hard part is being patient enough to wait for it. Trusting that God really does have "a proper time and procedure" for all things takes an incredible amount of faith. This is especially true if our "misery" is adding extra weight to an already difficult time of waiting. Yes, we can (often reluctantly) agree that all things are done in God's timing but what about coupling that with the reminder that all things are also done by God's procedure. You may find yourself in a situation right now and think, "I just do not know what to do!" Are you willing to wait for God to show you the proper time and procedure, even if that means denying yourself the privilege of making your own decisions? God is faithful to answer our plea for discernment in matters weighing heavily on us. He will reveal His time and His procedure, but are we going to be faithful to wait for it?

...and the wise heart will know the proper time and procedure. Ecc 8:5b

Your timing is perfection,
My timing leaves great need.
If I had my timing,
I'd still be but a seed.

My growth, it would be stunted,
My life would be so small,
The character within me,
Would be no character at all.

My timing, it is selfish,
It is all about me.
Your timing, it is endless,
And involves eternity.

My timing says, "It's too late!
All my options, they are gone!"
Your timing says, "Just please wait,
The wait when over, won't seem long."

My vision it is clouded,
I can see but just one side.
Yet your vision, it is shrouded,
With infinite angles of divine!

Your purpose is magnificent,
You recreate the wheel!
Your blessings, they are Heaven sent,
And the outcome is surreal!

Day 14
Wilderness Waste

...He will comfort all her waste places... Isaiah 51:3

Do you have any waste places? Places that are dry and desolate? In the stillness of the hour when you are alone with your thoughts, is there a place of disappointment, confusion, or fear that plagues you? It could be a place of strong emotion held captive by a multitude of difficult circumstances. Or maybe deep down you see yourself as a waste place, so dry and cracked by life's scorching heat that there is nothing that will moisten to the depth of your pain. Beloved, you are not wasted. The places that have been laid waste in your life are in need of comfort. They are in need of God's gentle watering, His gentle mending, and His gentle tending. Do not pray for the dryness to be instantly removed, but rather pray that it be soothed by the Comforter and transformed into a nourishing spring that will overflow into the lives of those around you.

Open your desert up to the Savior,
Invite Him to walk with you through, hand in hand.
The path under foot may be hard yet awhile,
But your wilderness laid waste will become His Eden again!

And her wilderness He will make like Eden, and her desert like the garden of the Lord; Joy and gladness will be found in her, thanksgiving and sound of melody. Isaiah 51:3, NASB

Day 15
God of the Plains

... Their gods are gods of the mountains, therefore they were stronger than we; but rather let us fight against them in the plain, and surely we shall be stronger than they. 1 Kings 20:23

We may have just encountered a battle so fierce that it was obvious to everyone, even ourselves that God was fighting on our behalf. It could have been the kind of life altering trial that the Lord not only prepared us for, but clearly carried us through so that even we were astounded at the outpouring of His mercy and His grace! However, just as with every mountaintop victory, there is eventually a descent back down into the plains, into the lowly valley. When the descent is made, the enemy begins to plan his next attack thinking, "I could not shake this child of God on the mountain, but surely I can take him/her down as they drudge through the valley of everyday life alone." It is in the valley where we begin to feel the throbbing ache from our previous battle's wounds. It is in the valley where our view is obstructed and we cannot physically see the glorious scenery which had been laid out before us on the mountain's peak. But are we to believe the enemy? Do we believe that our God is only a God of the mountain and not of the valleys also? That He will not fight for us in the plains just as powerfully as He did on the hills? Thankfully, we do not serve a "pull yourself up by your own bootstraps" kind of God. We are not ultimately alone in the valley, having to depend solely on our own strength just to make it through the day and night. The enemy may be planning his next attack but, God is already sending in His Heavenly forces, standing by, waiting for the command to fill our valley with His presence! The battle, whether won on the hills or down in the valley low, is always His!

... This is what the LORD says: 'Because [they] think the LORD is a god of the hills and not a god of the valleys, I will deliver this vast army into your hands, and you will know that I am the LORD.' 1 Kings 20:28, brackets mine

Oh dear Lord, when I'm a mess,
When the enemy lurks,
And my soul needs rest,
Remind me to call upon Your name,
Get out my sword, confront the shame.
Cling to all I know is true,
Shut out the lies,
Proclaim Your truth!
Lift up my voice with shouts of praise!
And with my hands to You, I'll raise!
Not be deceived to cower down,
To isolate or feel shut out!
To wallow in all the woes of life,
Thinking I'm the only one with strife!
But stand back up and say, "AMEN!"
My Savior overcomes and wins!
And I need never to be ashamed,
For who I am in Jesus Name!
For no matter what threatens me today,
My Jesus, My King, will have His way!
And He will always see me through,
He's a God of the hills and the valleys too!

Day 16
A Joyous Feast

When your words came, I ate them; they were my joy and my heart's delight, for I bear your name, LORD God Almighty. Jeremiah 15:16

Oh, the rich, satisfying, and savory Word of God! There is nowhere else where we can find such nourishment, such deep satisfaction other than within the pages of God's precious Word. They are worth feasting on! They are not only our soul's nourishment; they are life to our whole body. Yet, unless we digest God's Word, we are merely reading it as any other book on the shelf. On the contrary, it has got to become something we simply cannot live without! The Holy Spirit within us bears witness directly with the spoken Word of the Father. Therefore, we must allow the Spirit to plunge Scripture deep into the recesses of our soul, filling us so full that we are overflowing with overwhelming joy and sheer delight! A filling that quickens every cell in our body and causes our hearts to beat furiously with anticipation of a Divine encounter! It ought to be our life's calling to know Him, to want nothing more in this life but to be near Him, and to seek Him above all else. We must desire to honor His name in such a way that we simply cannot have a conversation without telling of His unfailing love and faithfulness to us! When Scripture becomes part of who we are, sharing Jesus with the world will become effortless!

Let's let the old adage, "You are what you eat"
become true for us according to Your Word, Lord!

Oh taste and see that the Lord is good!
His Word will never fail!
Sweet as honey to my mouth,
Ingest and savor the smell!
The rich aroma, the fragrance,
The nourishing well of truth,
Of all the things to be desired,
My joy and delight is proof!

Day 17
Undeniably God

When the LORD brought back the captive ones of Zion, we were like those who dream. Then our mouth was filled with laughter and our tongue with joyful shouting; then they said among the nations, "The LORD has done great things for them." The LORD has done great things for us; we are glad. Restore our captivity, O LORD, as the streams in the South. Psalm 126:1-4 (NASB)

What an exciting life; believing God for the unbelievable! Captive to our sin, captive to our circumstances, or simply captive to ourselves, once we are brought back to freedom, it is like a dream. An inexpressible joy and relief fills our mouths with laughter and our tongues with joyful shouting! If we have truly waited on the LORD alone, then we cannot deny that it was God Himself who engineered our every step and gloriously delivered us. Not only can we never deny it, but even those who look on will say, "The LORD has done great things for them!" Yes! *"The Lord has done great things for us; we are glad!"*

Restore our captivity, O LORD, as the streams in the South.
We have sought You on our faces, we've proclaimed You in this house!
In Your faithfulness You have brought us from a dark and captive place,
Your Sovereign hand undeniable, Your chosen ones, none disgraced!

Now our mouths are filled with laughter, our tongues with shouts of praise!
What the LORD God has accomplished, let no one bring to shame!
We honor You, Our King of Kings, we praise You all our days,
For the LORD has done great things for us, O let us count the ways!

Day 18
Invitation to Life

You Who have shown us [all], troubles great and sore, will quicken us again and will bring us up again from the depths of the earth. Psalm 71:20 (Amp)

Troubles great and sore are no respecter of persons, since they have been shown to us *all*. Notice here in the Psalm that it is God who has shown us these troubles. God will allow us to be buried under a heap of troubles just to show Himself mighty in our lives. These troubles bring us to a place of humility before our God. They force us to fully grasp our dependency on Him as we are painfully made aware of our weaknesses. Troubles beg us to reflect on our limitations and cry out for God to equip us with Divine power! Our troubles give us depth and sincerity as we consider that we are not the only ones being burdened by such griefs. And in our times of distress, there is no limit to the prayers that we are allowed and *urged* to offer to the LORD. For if it is He who exercises the right to allow such trouble, then it is also He who will *quicken us again*! If God has granted our afflictions access to the very depths of our soul, then they have only been given permission to clear a path for the Spirit's entrance. Once given undeniable admittance, they serve as one of our most valuable assets— an invitation to life!

...in all our troubles my joy knows no bounds.
2 Corinthians 7:4b

For I satisfy the weary ones and refresh everyone who languishes. Jeremiah 31:25

The demands of the day have brought me so low,
My spirit is downcast, nothing left here to sow.
Fatigue, strong emotions, have laid hold of me,
And there seems no hope, with a future unseen.
I am poured out like wine and broken apart,
All the pride of the day, stolen out of my heart.
I am weary and languished as I carry this load,
This burden You've given, I struggle to hold.
So with care and relief, on my face here again,
The brokenness I feel, will Your Spirit please mend?
Your mercy is what carries this heavy weight for me,
And with grace You will satisfy my each and every
need.
Now according to Your Word, I will be refreshed
once more,
Because despite what I feel, in my life, You are LORD!

Day 19
Worth Imitating

After all, though you should have ten thousand teachers (guides to direct you) in Christ, yet you do not have many fathers. For I became your father in Jesus Christ through the glad tidings (the Gospel). So I urge and implore you, be imitators of me. 1 Corinthians 4:15a-16, Amp

Now more than ever, the times call for fathers and mothers strong in the faith. Many young men and women are desperate for someone not only to follow, but to imitate. It is much easier to guide or to teach, rather than represent a solid, steady, self–disciplined man or woman in Christ, one which the younger generations want to emulate. Can we, as Paul, be bold enough to say, be an imitator of me? This requires us to walk closely with the Lord, knowing, understanding, and living by His Word. This requires us to become the person we were created in Christ to be (no matter what our age) and to be pure in word, spirit, and deed. There are young women plagued with insecurity, desperately needing to absorb the strength of another woman who is secure in Christ. And not only secure, but filled with joy rather than anxiety! A woman who is enjoying everyday life and despite the trials of life, has an anchor she not only talks about, but firmly holds onto. Younger generations need a man who has allowed the Holy Spirit to infiltrate every fiber of his being and is not satisfied with anything but Christ alone. A man with quiet confidence and strength, ready to give of himself to others because in Christ he lacks nothing. Holy Spirit, open our eyes and our hearts to the men and women around us who are in dire need of a father and mother in Christ. Then let us examine ourselves to see if we have allowed God to make us a guide worth following and emulating.

And so you became a model to all the believers...
1 Thessalonians 1:7

Whatever it takes, make us genuine,
Only a reflection of Thee.
Whatever it takes, may we not pretend,
That things are just as they seem.

Instead let us see the tender side,
Let us see the heart that aches.
Let us notice the one who is terrified,
Catching pieces as their heart breaks.

Help us understand the needy,
Help us understand the hurt.
Help us recognize the bleeding,
See the wounds as they're unearthed.

Show us how to be a model,
Not to please with tongue-in-cheek.
Not to excuse sin that we coddle,
Lest we fall, the flesh is weak.

In repentance, make us humble,
May believers in us see,
That the only way to model,
Is pleading, "Jesus, be seen in me!"

Day 20
Powerfully Dependent

But as for me, I am filled with power, with the Spirit of the Lord... Micah 3:8a

Oh, to be at a place where we can say in confidence, *"But as for me..!"* Micah was certain of his calling, certain of the power behind his message. We tend to be bound by life's uncertainty. It causes us to never fully grasp the power we possess through the indwelling Spirit of God. Uncertainty causes us to severely lack confidence in who we are in Christ. This often results in us placing security in ourselves to keep our minds momentarily at ease. Consequently, we end up becoming more independent of God, sacrificing His power to preserve such independence. Beloved, we will never be filled with power until we accept the uncertainty and claim total dependency on Christ because only in that dependency, do we find our true identity.

Beloved, we must ask ourselves,
Is Jesus more than enough?
Is He when Satan seems to prevail,
And our circumstances are tough?

Beloved we must ask ourselves,
Do we really trust the Lord?
Do we believe His Word never fails,
And can we pray in one accord?

Beloved, we must ask ourselves,
Can we fully surrender all?

Can we wait until His plan He unveils,
And then answer Him when He calls?

Oh Lord, let our amaze You,
Instead of the lack thereof!
Let our love and trust be so true,
As high are the heavens above!

Day 21
So Broken

Blessed are those who mourn, for they will be comforted.
Matthew 5:4

A heart so broken, things I don't understand.
An aching so painful, I cannot withstand.
A body so tired, fatigued from my grief.
A feeling so numbing, there seems no relief.
A mind so confused, left questioning all things.
A perplexity so despairing from such tragedy.
A soul so empty, parched from within.
A life so disturbed, where do we begin?

Yet...

A Presence so real, I cannot explain,
A soothing so deep, it will forever remain.
A Presence so near, I can almost touch.
A renewing so vital, when fatigue is much.
A Presence so steady, it anchors me still,
An imparting so intimate, communion I feel.
A Presence so full, my soul's thirst is met,
A confiding so sure, it leaves me no regret.

Day 22
Secure In His Silence

Let him sit alone in silence, for the LORD *has laid it on him.*
Lamentations 3:28

The silence given us by the Lord can often be discouraging. However, let us consider past seasons of willful disobedience. Once brought under the discipline of God, those seasons may have been graciously followed by the security of silence. Although, rather than seeing this period of silence as something secure, we may not have understood why we were dealt with in such a manner. But it is on these isles of isolation that we give way to God's authority, trusting and waiting for Him to speak to us. Seasons of sorrow may produce a similar period of calmness. Even in this, we see that God is merciful for He knows our hearts must ponder His ways and accept His Lordship over our lives. Yet, through both our seasons of sin and sorrow, such a silence from the Lord may still seem cold or withdrawn. Surely just the opposite is true! For the quietness placed on us is meant to draw us nearer to the heart of God. To be stripped away of everything we thought we knew about our Lord or even about ourselves. Then at last, once the silence is broken, upon hearing Him speak, we know we need only to be devoted to Jesus. And once *fully* devoted, the Holy Spirit has complete control to manifest God's glory and power in our lives without restraint! Beloved, this is something we must allow our Father to accomplish in us, for surely we cannot come to this place on our own.

Sweet friend, not forgotten, has this been laid on you,
This silence, this solitude, which He has handed to but
few?

Smoldering wick He will not quench, the reed He will
not break,
What He has planned to do through you, will be for
glory's sake.

So sit alone in silence, for the Lord has laid it on you,
Powerfully He is equipping you, as only He can do!

Day 23
Defeat the Beast

When my heart was grieved and my spirit embittered, I was senseless and ignorant; I was a brute beast before You. Psalm 73:21-22

Severely difficult circumstances do not usually bring out the "best" in us, but rather the "beast" in us. Notice that the attitude and action described by the psalmist is the result of anger and bitterness. First, his *heart was grieved;* something devastating could have caused this to happen which was beyond his control. Second, his *spirit embittered.* The sheer disappointment and confusion resulting from his grieved heart caused bitterness to take up residence in his spirit. Thus the manifestation played out in his actions toward God and probably toward those he loved as well: *I was senseless and ignorant; I was a brute beast before You.* If we find ourselves in this state, we are not without hope. In brokenness, the psalmist admitted his condition to the Lord. We also must recognize this condition in ourselves and desperately seek God for healing. If we rend our heart, fully exposing the sin that has manifested itself through our actions, then we can replace our anger and bitterness with truth. The beast in us can be defeated, but not without a fight. As practical as it may seem, write down every verse you can muster to combat whatever has brought you to this state of resentment. Sow the seed of God's Word in your heart. Read it, write it, meditate on it until the heart is healed, the bitterness gone, and the beast defeated! And most importantly, remember that we are not alone in our struggles!

Yet I am always with You; You hold me by my right hand. You guide me with Your counsel, and afterward You will take me into glory. Psalm 73:23-24

Day 24
Follow Not Your Heart

The heart is deceitful above all things, and desperately wicked: who can know it? Jeremiah 17:9, KJV

What a harsh reality this is! We may read this frightful verse and think it not to be entirely true of us. Could my heart really be that deceptive? Could it really be that wicked? Ah, but you see, in questioning this truth our heart has already begun to deceive us and pride comes to our defense. Who *can know it?* We simply cannot know it, therefore we must expose it fully to the Lord. In humility, we must accept that only God can search out our hearts to find the true motives and intentions. Do not be deceived, our natural tendency is to protect and harden our hearts in fear of being hurt or humiliated. But if we will relinquish what limited control we have, then we will find that the One who fashioned our heart will gently soften and conform it to His own.

If our hearts condemn us, we know that God is greater than our hearts, and He knows everything.
1 John 3:20

Who may ascend the mountain of the Lord? Who may stand in His holy place? The one who has clean hands and a pure heart...Psalm 24:3-4a

Lord, let me meditate on You,
For if I died today,
I would pray my heart be true,

Before I pass away.
So no matter what I'm facing,
May my heart be purified,
And while I'm still here waiting,
In my life, be glorified.

Day 25
Conscientious Consecration

The priests, however, were too few to skin all the burnt offerings; so their kinsmen the Levites helped them until the task was finished and until other priests had been consecrated, for the Levites had been more conscientious in consecrating themselves than the priests had been.
2 Chronicles 29:34

This account enlightens us to how the priests *were too few* to perform their duties because there was a lack of urgency in their consecration. Their procrastination resulted in having to hand over their responsibilities to their kinsmen, the Levites, until the rest of the priests were cleansed. It was the Levites who were *more conscientious in consecrating themselves than the priests had been.* Oh, how this can speak volumes to us! Although our sin has been atoned for by the blood of Jesus, we are still called to daily consecrate ourselves with the washing of the Word. We are still called to possess a humble spirit of repentance and daily confess our sins to the One who is faithful to forgive us. Oh, the simplicity of obedience to Christ! But have we become as the priests of Israel who were too comfortable in their position to conscientiously consecrate themselves? Let us make every effort to daily consecrate ourselves before the Lord in order to serve before Him as He has called us.

If we confess our sins, He is faithful and just and will forgive us our sins and purify us from all unrighteousness. 1 John 1:9

Anger and doubt reside in me,
Please cleanse me, Lord, and set me free.
And with Your fire, burn away,
The chaff in me that wants to stay.
Forgive my sins and wash me clean,
As I make confession my daily routine.
I confess anger, frustration, and unbelief,
For instead of these, it's submission You seek.
I confess selfishness, self-pity and if I ever think,
That Your arm is too short or even too weak.
So forgive me, Lord, of these I pray,
For truly I only want Your way,
And set me free, so that I will stay,
Seeking to be Christ—like this day.

Day 26
Near Your Altar

Even the sparrow has found a home and the swallow a nest for herself where she may raise her young, a place near Your altar, O LORD Almighty, my King, and my God. Psalm 84:3-4

O how sweet a melody, this little bird does sing,
Her young ones nestled tightly, underneath each feathered wing.
Her family safely settled, her children resting warm,
What a calming refuge she has found amidst the storm.

O yes! My heart rejoices as I see this tiny bird,
The melody she's singing, so beautifully is heard.
Yet I cannot help but wonder what makes her nest so sweet,
But this prayer now comes to me, lying at my Master's feet.

O Lord, just as this swallow makes her nest secure,
Let my home be as hers is, this blessing do ensure.
Joyfully I raise my young, under the shadow of Your wings,
And I lift my voice to Heaven, just as this swallow sings.

O Father, all I ask, is that I remain so close to Thee,
A refuge from my present storm, Your altar close to me!

Day 27
Nothing Left Undone

I will lead the blind by ways they have not known, along unfamiliar paths I will guide them; I will turn the darkness into light before them and make the rough places smooth. These are the things I will do and I will not leave them undone. Isaiah 41:16 (NIV, NASB)

In this verse, the Lord describes two ways He will guide us: *by ways we have not known* and *along unfamiliar paths*. Making the journey even more difficult is our lack of sight, *I will lead the blind…* What a comfort this is for those of us who feel as though God has left us in the dark, without a vision, without direction, and on a path that feels completely outside the realm of our comprehension. Why is this comforting? It is comforting because the Lord has done it. He has allowed circumstances to blind us to ways we would be tempted to lead ourselves. He has made the path so difficult to understand that nothing and no one other than the LORD Himself can guide us. Thus, we are called to take this unfamiliar way and if we understand that God has strategically planned our course, however dark and disappointing it may seem, we will witness His glory unfold right before our eyes. *I will turn the darkness into light before them and make the rough places smooth…* Our vision will be renewed and we will begin to see with clarity and vibrancy. The ground underfoot will invite us to take off our shoes and feel the now smooth path, the hard soil moistened, having been drenched with the dew of Heaven!

Keep walking, my friend, the darkness will dawn,
For these things He will do and will not leave undone!

Day 28
Treasures of Darkness

I will give you the treasures of darkness, riches stored in secret places, so that you may know that I am the LORD, the God of Israel, Who summons you by name. Isaiah 45:3

Oh, how this verse gives the promise of great plunders! We can gain so much more from our seasons of darkness than we realize if we will seek the Lord despite our feelings and despite our circumstances. Like a treasure buried deep within the darkest parts of the ocean, like the riches stored in the remotest locations, are the hidden gems of the Spirit! We should never emerge from our deserts without having drunk the water from the Rock and having eaten the manna from Heaven! God is so favorably disposed to those whose heart's desire is to know Him in the midst of their sufferings. If we focus on Christ when our souls are yearning and when our hearts are aching, He will satisfy us completely! We will know Him and love Him in a way we have never known before and when *He* summons us by name, we will respond!

The veil of darkness, thick with dread,
The path that I must take.
This season that brings sorrowful tears,
Must be, Lord, a mistake!

The frailty of my human heart,
The weakness of my flesh,
Reminds me there must be a way,
Must be a Victor in my stead!

And yet, He stands here with me,
Within the dreadful, darkened veil,
And begins to sweetly show me,
The way I must prevail!

I must gather up the treasures,
Hidden deep within the mote,
Of my present circumstances,
That seem to bind me under oath.

I must resist the tempter's vices,
Those of sloth and selfish need,
And see these gems of Heaven
Staring back at me!

I must drink the Rock's refreshment,
Taste of the manna nourishing,
Draw from eternity's investment,
Being stored up just for me!

Day 29
Do Not Be Silent!

But when I was silent and still, not even saying anything good, my anguish increased. Psalm 39:2

Satan will often hit us threefold when our circumstances have completely overwhelmed us. First, he will *sift* us (Luke 22:31). However, he knows that Jesus has already prayed for us, that our faith would not fail under such testing (22:32). So if the sift is not successful, Satan may try to *separate* us from our nearness and intimacy with Christ by tempting us to sin (Isaiah 59:2). Nevertheless, he knows that nothing can ultimately separate us from the love of Christ (Rom 8:39). Lastly, if neither sifting nor separating can turn us away from Christ, then maybe he can *silence* us in our anguish. This can often be the most detrimental of all three because if we are silenced in this way, we will be less likely to humble ourselves and pray—let alone be bold enough to proclaim the faithfulness of God to others. Not only will prayer and proclamation be held from our hearts and lips, but so will the power of praise! Satan knows that if he can intimidate us enough to give way to silence, then we will begin to isolate ourselves from God and from others. Such isolation will render us useless as a disciple of Christ. Satan cannot take away our salvation through the sifting, nor can he separate us from the love of Christ, but he can try to make us ineffective. Don't stay silent, my friend! Humble yourself in prayer, even amidst your anguish, then lift your voice in praise to our

Mighty King! Instead of letting the enemy silence us,
let the LORD silence our enemy!

*From the lips of children and infants you have
ordained praise because of your enemies, to silence
the foe and the avenger. Psalm 8:2*

*In your unfailing love, silence my enemies; destroy all
my foes, for I am your servant. Psalm 143:12*

*For every precious promise,
For every powerful Word,
Every prayer that we have uttered,
In Your mercy, You have heard!*

*And You answer so completely,
Filling in all that we lack,
Allowing us this special privilege,
To see You move and act!*

*For Satan wants us silent,
To forget just Whose we are!
Forget we are the children,
Of a Sovereign, powerful God!*

*Of the King of all the nations,
Of the Creator of the Earth,
Of the Universe and Heavens,
The Blessed Lifter of the curse!*

*So fear not, my beloved,
When Your Goliath starts to taunt,
For the armies of the Living God,
Will he defy? No! He will not!*

Day 30
I Am Convinced

...I know whom I have believed and am convinced that He is able... 2 Timothy 1:12b

Surging waves of uncertainty almost always accompany the storms we face in our lives. The most inconceivable of circumstances surrounding our present trial can manifest such waves, leaving us literally nauseated. Once the wave has subsided, although our trial may still be present, we are at least able to bring our head above water and breathe. But what if the waves just keep rolling in? What if there is no temporary relief and you feel as though you will certainly drown? What if you see no way out and even all the praying and crying out to God still leaves you paralyzed? What then? The answer...breathe anyway! Even if you are completely under water, just breathe as if you were given supernatural gills like the creatures of the sea! Then open your eyes to the Creator of the Universe and whisper sweetly to Him, *"I know Whom I have believed. I do not know the complexity of my circumstances, but I know Whom I have believed and You, O Sovereign One, are able! Yes, You are able to enable me to breathe under water!"* Just when we think there is no way out, we see that it is God who is doing the inconceivable in our lives!

When I feel I'm drowning,
And I cannot go on,
I lift my hands toward Heaven,
Though I cannot hold for long.

You seem to let me flounder,
To let me sink beneath,
The waters of uncertainty,
And there seems no relief!
Yet in this state of panic,
I hear You say to me,
"You can breathe, My child,
Breathe here in the deep!"

Day 31
The Ancient Path

This is what the LORD says: 'Stand at the crossroads and look; ask for the ancient paths, ask where the good way is, and walk in it, and you will find rest for your souls...' Jeremiah 6:16a

Is this where you stand, my friend, at the crossroads of your current situation? Is there is no clear direction for the next step you are to take, the next path you are to travel? As you stand at this crossroads, you may see many paths, but which one are you to take? It could be that you have traveled some of these paths before and although they brought you to a destination, they did not bring *rest for your soul*. So here you stand and around you look. Notice that the LORD has not asked you to pick the path that seems logical or the path that seems clear cut. In fact, the LORD has not asked you to pick at all. You are to ask Him for the *ancient path*. The path that He has already traveled, the path that He has already laid out for you. This ancient path has been traveled by saints before you. It has been walked on by weary souls and provided them rest under its weeping willows and shady oaks. This ancient path has seen many storms which have only strengthened and nourished it with heavy rains and strong billowing winds. This, my friend, is the path you are to walk in, for this ancient path leads to the Ancient of Days! Ask Him and He will lead you. And there, you will find rest for your soul.

Lead me Lord, I want to know,

This ancient path, O please do show.
These other ways seem familiar to me,
But I desire the path that's been traveled by Thee.

Though I am traveling, my soul needs rest,
And if You will show me, I know I'll be blest.
But Lord, Your blessings are not all I seek,
I want only the path that will lead to Your feet.

I'm now at the crossroads, I'm ready to leave,
Though to Your presence, I resign to cleave.
I need no compass, for I trust in Your hand,
And when this journey is over, in Bethel I'll stand!

Day 32
Perfect Possessions

Every good gift and every perfect gift is from above and cometh down from the Father... James 1:17a, KJV

How treasured we are by our Heavenly Husband, who is also our Heavenly Father! He gives us good gifts, tangible and material gifts provided through human means, which bring us joy and provide for our basic needs. And not only do we receive good gifts of provision, but so often He bestows on us gifts that satisfy our material *wants*. Graciously, He does not limit His gifting with only good gifts, for we see that we are also given *perfect* gifts! Perfect gifts are gifts that leave us so completely satisfied that our soul lacks nothing. These gifts, bountiful gifts are in themselves overflowing with multiple blessings! Perfect gifts were created for us from the beginning of time and exude the essence of newness, remaining fresh within us for all eternity. Oh Lord, how we then marvel at the exquisite gift of salvation! The completeness of this gift being perfected within us! The perfection of what is now our possession in Christ! We simply cannot measure this bounty, this benefaction freely bestowed on us. Truly it has made us anew and recreated us to find our completeness in the One who descended from above!

Oh, this bounty, this benefaction, this perfect gift received!
The wealth of Christ's salvation stored up when we believe!

Lord open up the floodgates, and let Your good gifts
flow,
Then open up our hearts to receive all You'll bestow!
We know that every perfect gift comes to us from
You,
And never will we doubt all that Your Word says You
will do!
You are the Giver of all things wonderful, seen and
unseen here,
Our flesh, our soul lacks nothing and our hearts shall
never fear!
So we raise our hands to Heaven, to the Giver from
above,
Who gave His all, His everything, so we could
experience His love!

Day 33
My Story

Let us fix our eyes on Jesus, the author and perfecter of our faith... Hebrews 12:2a

Here we see such a wonderful description of who Jesus is for us. He is the *Author*, writing the story of our lives! He alone knows the beginning and the end of our story, perfecting every detail in between so that our faith will be proved genuine. Oh, to trust Him more! If we really believed He was the One doing all the writing, we would rest in His sovereign knowledge and creative authorship. We would not only trust Him from beginning to end, but would give Him the liberty to be so wonderfully creative with each and every detail in between. If we let Him, Jesus will write us a biography so intriguing, so exciting and so mysterious, that readers would look forward to each new chapter with great anticipation! Dear friend, let Him have the pen! Resist trying to write your own story out of fear of the unknown. Notice also that here in this verse, we are given our life's calling and that is to *fix our eyes on Jesus*. Not fix our eyes on ourselves and what we can do, but fix our eyes on Him. One sentence written by the finger of God can change the course of history! So rather than be the author of your own life, offer yourself to Jesus everyday as a blank sheet of paper and let Him write your story.

Perfect submission, all is at rest;
I in my Savior am happy and blest,
watching and waiting, looking above,

filled with His goodness, lost in His love.

This is my story, this is my song,
Praising my Savior, all the day long.
This is my story, this is my song,
Praising my Savior, all the day long!

Blessed Assurance, Hymn
Fanny Crosby, 1873

Day 34

Remembering Your Faithfulness

My soul is downcast within me; therefore I will remember You from the land of the Jordan, the heights of Hermon — from Mount Mizar. Psalm 42:5b

O Lord, my soul is downcast, my heart heavy within me,
Life's wild torrents and raging waves, dragging me out to sea!
This Psalmist seemed to have shared, a similar, downcast state,
So what shall I glean from his message, his deep and sincere heartache?
"Yes, this Psalmist's soul has been tested, tried, and abused.
It had seen misery unspeakable and his people violently accused.
But this Psalmist whose soul cried out, in anguish, seeking only Me,
Is the very servant I chose to use, for the message you now read.
Child I know that you are aching, you are weary, yes indeed,
But let us consider together, that I am here to meet your need.
This Psalmist gazed out at the Jordan, a river so deep, so vast,
And thus remembered the nourishment, I had given him in the past.
Then he looked to the heights of Hermon, one of the tallest of peaks,

And remembered happy, joyous times, the festivals lasting for weeks.
Last he fixed on Mount Mizar, maybe a small and mundane hill,
But at this sight he remembered, that I have kept him in My will.
So when you are discouraged, your soul in dire straight,
Look at this verse and ponder, then look to Me, and wait.
Remember how I have nourished your soul, any dryness long forgot.
Then think back to all My faithfulness after many prayers were sought.
I know your soul is downcast, but My Spirit is thriving within,
Come to Me and I'll remind you where we're going and where we've been!"

Day 35
Revealer of Mysteries

...Surely your God is the God of gods and the Lord of kings and a Revealer of Mysteries... Daniel 2:47

The book of Daniel is one of the most captivating, thrilling, gut-wrenching books of the Bible! Nowhere else do we see God named as a *Revealer of Mysteries* as we do in this minor prophetic book. And yet, was not Daniel's own life a mystery in itself? Although born into the royal family of Israelites, even his noble birth could not keep him from captivity to the great king of Babylon. Nevertheless, even in such extreme circumstances, he held fast to his convictions and remained available for God to use in any way He saw fit. The *Revealer of Mysteries* not only revealed great visions to Daniel, He revealed Himself! He proved to Daniel that He was a God worthy of his unhindered obedience, worthy of his confidence, and worthy of his life. If we, like Daniel, give our lives over to the Lord in strict obedience, confident faith, and sacrificial devotion, we too can be available for Him to use in profound ways. If we are held captive by what seem like life's unfortunate circumstances, there is still a *Revealer of Mysteries* whose glory can shine forth through us, even amidst the darkest of days!

Although life may seem mysterious,
With each strenuous, passing day;
There is a Revealer of Mysteries,
His Sovereignty guiding you all the way.
Although it may be difficult,

You cannot see the result of His plan;
The Revealer of Mysteries has more to unveil,
So much more than you understand.
Although captivity may be your home,
With no comforts from your past.
Hold true to your convictions,
And His glory He will unmask!

Day 36
The Heart Speaks

My heart says of You, "Seek His face!" Your face, LORD, I will seek. Psalm 27:8

Does not this verse put into words the longing in our hearts! What does your heart tell you to seek? Truly we cannot discern our discontentment unless we listen to our hearts' cry for the remedy. The constant activity around us can hush the gentle whisper of the Spirit and only solitude and silence can quicken us to hear it once again. Oh, the sweetness of solitude! It quiets our minds and lets our hearts speak to our true Love. It reminds us that we are not really alone but instead, lingering in Heavenly fellowship with our souls suspended between Heaven and earth! Dear friend, do not put off time spent in solitude with your Savior. His heart longs to meet with you. Will you not respond to your heart's tender proposal to seek His face? *My heart says of You, "Seek His face!" Your face, LORD, I will seek.*

Quietly alone I sit, resting each busy and anxious thought;
Here I am to seek Your face, temptations to fidget are fought.

Solitude, sweet solitude, I begin to hear my heart speak,
To the longings, to the frustrations, known to make my spirit weak.

Since there's no one else to listen, honest my heart can be.
No one to take my attention, so fully I give it to Thee.

Another day upon me, my heart's longings never cease,
But now I discern His calling, His whisper brings clarity and peace.

"Seek My face" is what I hear, these words so clear to me!
"Seek His face," the cry of my heart! Yes, I know it forever will be!

Day 37
Drawing Deep

Counsel in the heart of man is like water in a deep well, but a man of understanding draws it out. Proverbs 20:5

There is a rich store of wisdom and knowledge that resides deep within our hearts. If we have pondered or meditated on Scripture to any degree, then our hearts have been given counsel. God's Word is so alive and active within us that when we begin to call on the name of the Lord, He will answer us out of the well of the Word living inside us. Truly He is our Counselor! How much more will we have to draw from when we are continually asking for His filling! Daily ask for the pouring out of the Holy Spirit and daily fill up on the Word of God. However, it is not enough only to be filled, we must also draw from those fillings. Therefore, remember to take a ladle to the well of your soul in your times of desperation. Dip into the counsel within, moment by moment, upon every endeavor, in every relationship, and in all things. The Spirit of God within you will keep you rightly related to Jesus with every step you take and every decision you make. You need only to draw out of the depths of the riches of Christ's salvation!

Draw deep, dear soul, His counsel is there,
Your ladle He'll fill, as you whisper each prayer!

As He fills your soul, His blessings release,
He heals the heart, bringing sweet relief.

He measures His Spirit not by standards today,

But instead overflows in His generous way!

And He'll never withhold His mercies from you,
But instead bring fresh showers, each morning anew!

Day 38
Revelation Through Reverence

The secret of the Lord is with them that fear Him; and He will show them His covenant. Psalm 25:14, KJV

This verse ought to incite us to place the reverence for the holiness of God as a high priority in our everyday lives. Oh, if we would ponder the King of Kings, high and lifted up, seated on His throne, accompanied by an angelic host too numerous to count! Then we too may find ourselves as the elders on their faces crying, "Holy, Holy, Holy!" *The secret of the Lord is with those who fear Him...* Do you want to know His secrets? Do you long and yearn for the deep, hidden treasures of your relationship in Christ? Do you desire intimacy with the only One whose relationship brings complete satisfaction? The mysteries of the covenant, given to us through Christ's propitiation for our sin, will only be revealed when we have rid ourselves of all our pride. When we have reverently bowed everything we are and given all we have to our King. Yes, we receive His salvation if we believe Christ to be the Son of God and the only means for our souls to live eternally with the Father. But do we stop there? There are many secrets waiting to be revealed to the one whose life is lived in *full* submission— trusting, waiting, and anticipating to hear God's voice and see His face!

The secret [of the sweet, satisfying companionship] of the Lord have they who fear —revere and worship— Him, and He will show them His covenant, and reveal to them its [deep, inner] meaning. Psalm 25:14, Amplified Bible

Day 39
Sowing Tears

Those who sow in tears will reap with songs of joy. He who goes out weeping, carrying seed to sow, will return with songs of joy, carrying sheaves with him. Psalm 126:5-6

What a promise of restoration amidst the sorrow we experience in this life! Only with Christ can our tears be sown into the soil of Heaven, allowing us to reap the fruit of the Spirit with songs of joy! Just imagine Christ's gentle hands gathering our tears, taking them away and returning to us the sheaves of His overwhelming presence. We must go out weeping, carrying the seed of His Word, trusting it to be fulfilled in our lives and in eternity. And even in our deepest sorrows, the greatest blessing is to carry the seed to others, being vulnerable enough to allow the grace of God to shine forth through us. Once we have scattered seeds through our sorrows, we will begin to see that we have reaped a heart full of praise and adoration for our great Comforter, who in turn, makes us a comfort to others.

Lord, in my times of heartbreak,
When I don't understand,
When life is more than I can take,
And I'm sinking in the sand.

That's when You remind me,
Child, "Sow My Word!
Deep into your broken heart,
Eternal echoes heard!"

"And as You sow each promise,
Water them with your tears,
Then what you reap, will nourish,
Hurting souls to come, for years!"

Day 40
Stuck in the Mud

They lowered Jeremiah by ropes into the cistern; it had no water in it, only mud and Jeremiah sank down into the mud.
Jeremiah 38:6b

Jeremiah, one of the most well—known prophets of the Old Testament, was mocked, beaten, imprisoned, and now here he is, *stuck in the mud*! All this for doing what God had called him to do. Beloved, has God called you to serve Him yet you find yourself stuck in the mud and sinking? You may be in a dry and desperate place with no joy, let alone the energy to even crack a smile. I am convinced that God's greatest servants are those who find merriment in the mire! And while in a cistern of sorts, viewing our situation in a more light—hearted manner, may stop us from sinking even further! Those who believe that God's purpose will *never* fail and that He will fulfill every good work in their lives according to His Word, are those who can rest, even in the muddiest of circumstances. We never know how long God will allow us to be stuck in the mud, but if we find ourselves in such a place, let us pray that we will faithfully trust Him to *gently* pull us up!

Dirty distractions aside,
Lift your head and smile,
The length of your stay,
Is but only awhile!

...Put these old rags and worn—out clothes under your arms to pad the ropes. Jeremiah did so and they

pulled him up with the ropes and lifted him out of the cistern... Jeremiah 38:12b-13a

Day 41
The Midnight Cry!

The bridegroom was a long time in coming, and they all became drowsy and fell asleep. At midnight the cry rang out: 'Here's the bridegroom! Come out to meet him!' Matthew 25:5-6

Wake up, O Virgin Daughter, clothed with the purity of Christ!
Wake up, make ready and oil your lamp, let it burn now ever so bright!
Sleep not, thy soul, for know we not, when our redemption draweth near.
Be not weary in doing good; let your heart not give way to fear.
Wake up, O Daughter and seek your Groom, He is making ready the feast.
A wedding supper arrayed with splendor, where rejoicing will never cease!
Sleep not, though your Bridegroom may be delayed, away He will not stay.
Sleep not, though your sorrows be heavy, yet to doubting, do not give way.
Wake up! Can you hear it? The midnight cry, the shout from Zion has come!
Hallelujah! Hosanna! There in the clouds, the Bridegroom, the victory won!
Come out! Dear Bride, clothed in robes of Heaven, rise to meet your King!
Glory! All praise to the Lamb of God! Ten thousand, we join in and sing!
Worth the wait just to see His face, what a glory we now behold!

*Humbly, we kneel before our King, on our brow
placed a crown of pure gold!
Together at last with loved ones, all our sorrows
eternally ceased,
Sitting and sharing, tears wiped away, partake now in
the Heavenly feast!*

Day 42
Softened As We Wait

Ten days later the word of the LORD came... Jeremiah 42:7

No matter how many devotions, studies, books, and verses we read about waiting, it is still a challenge. What if God gave us a set time that He would answer us? Oh, how much easier would the wait be! Even one day can seem like eternity as we wait on God to give us the answer we so desperately need to hear. But look to our verse for today. *The word of the Lord came ten days later.* Did Jeremiah know the Lord would answer him a full ten days after he prayed? No, but he did know the Lord would answer. And why should Scripture give us this bit of information as to how long the wait, when in so many other instances, we are merely told, *the word of the Lord came?* Oh believer, wait in expectation with no deadline in mind! We know how hard it is to wait, but our gracious Heavenly Father reminds us that each day of waiting prepares us for our response to the answer we are about to receive. And if we read the above verse in the context of its chapter, these *ten days* allowed God's people to cultivate a submissive heart in their response to His answer. Unfortunately, instead of softening in those days of waiting, the people's hearts became hard and calloused toward God and they did not act in obedience to His word, once it finally came. Let us not be this way! Waiting prepares us for the response we will give to the answer we seek once it is given. So let this be of us, that the longer the wait,

the softer our hearts—being submissively receptive to
His answer to our prayers.

I just want the answer,
I want "Yes" or "No,"
I want You to say, "Stay here,"
I want You to say, "Go!"
I want to know the future,
I want to plan ahead,
I want to know the places,
Where my feet will tread.
I want to have the vision,
Of all that I will be,
Of what I can do just for You,
Of all my eyes can see!
But this is not Your way, Lord,
No not Your way at all!
Your plans, You keep them hidden,
Or else we'd never grow.
In waiting here, You teach us,
Teach us a fierce dependency!
In waiting here, You lead us,
Or else we'd run ahead of Thee.
So help me to be still, Lord,
To wait so patiently.
Even when I start to panic,
With a whisper, set me free.
And I'll stay here, calm, collected,
I'll focus on today,
Knowing You are always near me,
Giving the strength right now to wait!

Day 43

Love and Faith

Now faith is being sure of what we hope for and certain of what we do not see... Though you have not seen Him, you love Him; and even though you do not see Him now, you believe in Him and are filled with an inexpressible and glorious joy, for you are receiving the goal of your faith, the salvation of your souls. Hebrews 11:1, 1 Peter 1:8-9

Beloved, are you *receiving the goal of your faith?* What a blessed rest to know that our faith is directly related to our love for Christ. It is in Him, knowing Him and loving Him, that we *are filled with an inexpressible and glorious joy.* This, my friend, is the goal of our faith, the salvation of our souls. Our faith is not strengthened by acts of service, earthly relationships, pious living, or secured positions. *Now faith is being sure of what we hope for and certain of what we do not see. Though you have not seen Him, you love Him; and even though you do not see Him now, you believe in Him.* In seeking to love Him who is unseen, our faith will be strengthened beyond earthly measure! By the same token, the more we begin to understand the character of Christ and the sacrificial love He has for us, the stronger our faith and trust will be in Him. His Sovereignty, His mercy, His grace, His compassion, His righteousness, His faithfulness, His holiness, and His love. Everything He is, will compel us to surrender everything we are to Christ alone. And when His Divine character, through the miraculous workings of the Holy Spirit, begins to

replace ours, what an inexpressible and glorious joy
we will experience!

The three most important things to have are faith,
hope and love. But the greatest of them is love.
1 Corinthians 13:13

I searched the earth, far and wide,
To find the jewels of faith.
Where, pray tell, do these treasures hide,
Beyond the reach of my embrace?
I searched the Scriptures, the Holy Word,
What promises I have found!
Ah yes, salvation my ears have heard,
My soul now Heaven bound!
But still my faith is lacking,
Disappointed I must seem.
Day in, day out, the enemy attacking,
Failure part of my daily regime.
But alas, my heart is broken,
I've surrendered all my pride.
And there seems left not a token,
Of my character inside.
"This is exactly where I want you,"
His voice a whisper sweet.
"Empty now and in full view,
For love and faith to meet."
Oh Lord, what joy I now possess,
My despairing soul is gone!
Inexpressible is this blessed rest,
My heart sings a brand new song!
Faith is what we hope for,
And what we cannot see.
Faith is when we love Him more,
From the broken heart He's freed!

Day 44
Everlasting Consolation

Now the Lord Jesus Christ Himself, and God, even our Father, which hath loved us, and hath given us everlasting consolation... 2 Thessalonians 2:16, KJV

Everlasting consolation,
My every wound is healed,
In His death and resurrection,
Salvation is revealed!

Everlasting consolation,
My needless strivings cease.
In the shadow of His mighty wings,
Power and strength, will He release.

Everlasting consolation,
My tears are gently dried,
In the security of His abundant love,
Nowhere else, shall I abide.

Everlasting consolation,
His grace imparted unto me,
In the arms of my dear Savior,
I know Jesus is all I need.

Everlasting consolation,
Perfect rest, my soul does find.
In the presence of the risen King,
His glory is sublime!

Day 45
Challenged, Committed, Convicted, Changed

Therefore, since we have confidence to enter the Most Holy Place by the blood of Jesus, by a new and living way opened for us through the curtain, that is, His body, and since we have a great priest over the house of God, let us draw near to God with a sincere heart in full assurance of faith, having our hearts sprinkled to cleanse us from a guilty conscience and having our bodies washed with pure water. Hebrews 10:19-22

In my NIV Bible, the summary under which Hebrews 10:19 is written is titled, "A Call to Persevere." Your Bible may have this same title or something similar to it, but let's focus on the above verses truly being for us, *A Call to Persevere!* Although, before we can answer this call, we must fully understand its meaning. First, what is the call? We find it in verse 22; *let us draw near to God with a sincere heart in full assurance of faith.* Second, why do we draw near? Verse 19 tells us we draw near because *we have confidence to enter the Most Holy Place.* Third, how do we draw near? Also in verse 19, we draw near *by the blood of Jesus, by a new and living way opened for us through the curtain, that is, His body,* Christ's death on the cross. And because of Christ's death, there need not be another sacrifice for sin or another priest to be the mediator between God and man. Christ is now the *Great Priest over the house of God* (10:21). Lastly, what takes place when we draw near? *Our hearts are sprinkled to cleanse us from a guilty conscience and our bodies washed with pure water* (10:22). Over two thousand years ago,

Christ opened a *new and living way* for us to approach the throne of God in the Most Holy Place by His death and resurrection. We can now confidently draw near to God because of what he has done for us! So why are we not drawing near? Why do days go by and we do not enter into the Most Holy Place? This is our call, a call to persevere and draw near to God by spending time in His Word, in His Sanctuary, and in His Presence! Jesus Christ sacrificed everything so that in Him we would lack nothing. Therefore, draw near daily and be challenged, committed, convicted, and changed!

Challenged, my heart's true longing, is to be so near to You,
Committed, knowing nothing else, or better, can I do.
Convicted, as I humbly approach Thy blessed, Most Holy Place,
Changed, for now I hear Your voice and will one day see Your face!

Day 46

Today

But encourage one another daily, as long as it is called Today... Hebrews 3:13

Teach us, Lord, from this day forth,
To number all our days;
Apply our hearts to wisdom,
As we seek to know Your ways.
Help us, Lord, encourage each other,
For it is still Today.
May our hearts be stirred and allow Your Word,
To utterly amaze!
Guide us, Lord, into all Your truth,
Without You, we are lost.
May we discern the Spirit's leading,
And veer not, lest we count the cost.
Show us, Lord, Your glory,
As each day brings forth Your light.
We trust that You will cause us to shine,
Even in the darkest of night.
Bring us, Lord, into Your presence,
For we are weary indeed.
May we be encouraged, once again
To go forth and plant the seed!

Day 47

Reverent Submission

During the days of Jesus' life on earth, He offered up prayers and petitions with loud cries and tears to the One who could save Him from death, and He was heard because of His reverent submission. Hebrews 5:7

Can you even begin to imagine the power in the prayers offered up by Jesus to God the Father while He walked upon this earth? We get a glimpse of how He prayed here in this verse: *"He offered up prayers and petitions with loud cries and tears..."* There was never a question of Jesus' faith in the One He was praying to; neither was there even the slightest hint of unbelief! Knowing there is only One God, being the fullness of that One God in bodily form Himself, He still offered up His prayers on behalf of all Creation with *loud cries and tears to the One who could save Him from death.* Jesus allowed His life to be utterly dependent upon God the Father, even to the point of death. And why was He always heard when He prayed so fervently? *...because of His reverent submission.* By His example, are we not also to be solely dependent upon Christ, even to the point of death? Shall we not approach the Heavenly throne, in which Christ is seated at the right hand of God, with undeniable, unquestionable, and reverent submission? Let us examine ourselves before we offer up our prayers and petitions to the Lord. May they be submitted from a humble heart that is genuinely seeking the aid of the only One who has saved us from death!

Day 48
He Knows

But He knows the way that I take; when He has tested me, I will come forth as gold. Job 23:10

What an eternal comfort to fully believe that, *He knows the way I take!* Christ is all too familiar with our life's journey from birth until now. He has seen it from beginning to end. What He has started in us, even before we said "yes" to Jesus, He will complete in ways that our minds simply cannot conceive. Even when our trials seem to have no earthly value to us, God has already infiltrated their design into the fabric of our character to use for His eternal glory. Can we dare to be like Job and say with confidence, "He knows the way I take!" Can we also be as Job and believe that God will allow us to be tested so that our faith will be worth its weight in gold? He knows, my dear friend! He knows the way, the difficult way we are often asked to take and He has a purpose in it all. Keep walking steadily in the way He has directed you and place your confidence in the Refiner of your faith.

You know the way I take, Lord, I need not be afraid. So test on by Your Sovereign hand, till Thy glory be displayed!

Day 49
Heaven's Song

By the rivers of Babylon we sat and wept... There on the poplars we hung our harps... How can we sing the songs of the LORD while in a foreign land? Psalm 137:1-2, 4

Does this describe you, dear friend, as you sit beside your river of sorrow, having hung your harp of joy upon a weeping willow, wondering how you will ever sing songs of genuine praise to the Lord again? Have you been brought to a foreign land through your current trial and you now no longer possess the desire for worship? Maybe your relationship with the Lord seems to be devoid of fellowship because your trial has shown no mercy and taken every ounce of your strength. And even prayer seems like an added task with seemingly no promise of a return. You may think that now I will tell you to pick back up your instrument of joy and play a song anyway, despite how you feel. No, dear soul, I will not relay such a message to you today. What I will encourage you to do is remain seated and leave the harp on the tree. But as you sit, incline your ear instead to hear the song being sung around you.

Listen to the river's current, gently passing by.
Hear the leaves swing back and forth, gripped tightly to the vine.
Listen to the sparrow, rustling feathers in her nest.
Hear the pine trees swaying, standing taller than the rest.

Creation's always singing to her beloved Sovereign King,
It's a song of revelation, for the promises unseen.
Weary traveler, do you hear it, as you sit beside this stream?
Let your heart and harp find rest and on your Savior's bosom lean.
While creation still is singing, there's another song to hear,
If you listen rather closely you'll find Heaven very near.
It's a chorus of ten thousands, singing songs of the redeemed,
Their trials long forgotten, seeing glories never dreamed!
When the joy once in your heart, has been stolen all away,
Know the Master has His songs to sing over you this day.
Sit still beside the water and trust His Sovereign hand,
For one day you will sing again, even in this foreign land!

Day 50
A Great Recognition

...in order that sin might be recognized as sin... Romans 7:13b

The ability to *recognize sin as sin* in a person's life must be accomplished through the supernatural workings of the Holy Spirit. When, in repentance, we first come to Christ for salvation, the Spirit's conviction begins to operate within our soul. We then begin to see our sin nature for the filth that it is and desperately call on the name of Jesus to save us! Once we accept the price paid for such a great sin debt, we then seek to live lives of humble gratitude to a loving, righteous Savior. Nevertheless, once saved, our recognition of sin ought to only become greater with each passing day. Our sensitivity to sin must be so heightened that we dare not approach it for fear of regressing back to the very nature from which we are being saved. Let us never be caught saying, "What sin, Lord?" simply because we do not recognize it! Until we see our sin for what it really is, we cannot possess the power to overcome it. We often sugar coat our sin and therefore limit the Spirit's power within us to completely rid us of it once and for all. If we could admit that even our petty selfishness is as tragic a sin in the sight of God as the worst of crimes, maybe we would be on our faces in heart—rending confession. What a glorious humility would then replace our pride and selfishness once we were rid of it! We must remember that daily confession of sin leads to daily victory over sin!

Help us, Lord, to recognize, our each and every sin,

Knowing in repentance, that the flesh will cease to win!

Day 51
Not Worthy

Lord, I do not deserve to have You come under my roof...
Matthew 8:8

Do we deserve anything that we have been given in Christ? Can you think of anything that merits His mercy poured out on us? Oh, how He loves us, a people so undeserving! I cannot imagine that when we see His face, how we will be able to even stand in the presence of such Holiness. Paralyzed, we will likely fall to our face and say, "Lord, I don't deserve this!" Yet, He lifts us up, crowns us with glory and gives us a new name. He makes us sons and daughters of a Sovereign King and gives us an eternal inheritance, which He has kept for us from the beginning of time. *Lord, I do not deserve to have You come under my roof!* But thank You for entering into this desolate wasteland and filling it with an abundance of new life! Oh no, we will never deserve to have Him come to us, but He does so anyway.

I swept the house, so good and clean,
No speck of dust, found any a beam.
And I set out all my finest things,
Even polished all my napkin rings!
Why yes! I have a guest today,
And my plan is such to ask His stay!
Oh, what a calling this must be,
For He has asked to come see me!
The time is getting closer now,
Yes, He'll arrive, but not sure how?

Maybe He'll just knock at my door,
Or suddenly be standing on the kitchen floor!
What's this I feel, a gentle breeze?
I have to say, it startled me!
For suddenly I grew so faint,
Feeling anything, but a godly saint.
Instantly, I am not the same,
For all I feel is so much shame!
I better change my plans, oh no,
He can't come here, and see me so!
"Lord, no! Don't come here, under my roof!
I don't deserve this, Your Spirit's proof!
There is still so much I need to clean,
I can't possibly let You in to see!"
"My child, I've already let Myself in,
My Spirit is working to cleanse you of sin.
There really is nothing more you can do,
Just sit here beside Me and I'll talk with you."
"Yes, Lord, I will sit here, for You are all I seek,
Though not here beside You, instead at Your feet.
I'll never deserve what You've just done for me,
So with my life let me serve You, for all eternity."

Day 52
This Present House

When the builders laid the foundation of the temple of the LORD, the priests in their vestments and with trumpets, and the Levites (the sons of Asaph) with cymbals, took their places to praise the LORD, as prescribed by David, King of Israel. With praise and thanksgiving they sang to the LORD: "He is good; His love to Israel endures forever." And all the people gave a great shout of praise to the LORD, because the foundation of the house of the LORD was laid. But many of the older priests and Levites and family heads, who had seen the former temple, wept aloud when they saw the foundation of this temple being laid, while many others shouted for joy. Ezra 3:10-12

What a glorious celebration of thanksgiving! The exiles of Babylon were finally given the opportunity to return to Jerusalem and begin rebuilding the temple. Even before the walls were erected, they took their place to praise the Lord, dressed in vestments with trumpets and cymbals in hand! They praised the Lord because the foundation had been laid. They praised the Lord for the work He had begun, trusting its completion. Some danced and sang for joy at the sight of the new temple foundation. Yet others, who had seen the former temple, wept aloud. They remembered a better time, a time before their captivity, a time when the glory of the Lord dwelt in the temple built by King David's son. To them, the building of a new temple would never compare to the one their captors had reduced to rubble. Similar to the old priests and

Levites and family heads, do you find yourself weeping while others rejoice in thanksgiving? Do you long for the former days? You may see a new foundation being laid in your life but cannot possibly imagine it to be as wonderful as it was before. Precious friend, God knows the aching of your heart, just as He did these veterans of Israel, who ached for the former temple. Yet even in their longings, He promised them, *The glory of this present house will be greater than the glory of the former house,' says the LORD Almighty, 'And in this place I will grant peace...' Haggai 2:9.* Oh, how that promise extends to us!

Oh Lord, your children dance and sing,
They see Your works, giving thanksgiving!
But while they praise, some sadness looms,
For a temple which once held Heavenly rooms.
Just as today, hearts rejoice, others break,
For what could have been, without life's mistakes.
If only the former had still remained,
Surely joy and peace would our hearts have sustained.

Lord, help us to envision new walls being built,
Since our foundation stands firm, through Your blood that was spilt.
For there is yet a great blessing which we shall behold,
A temple of glory, laden with gold!
But until that grand day, let us new visions receive,
And with thanksgiving let us praise You and all Your promises believe!

Day 53
False Accusations

Then He showed me Joshua the high priest standing before the angel of the LORD, and Satan standing at his right side to accuse him. Zechariah 3:1

In a vision given to the prophet Zechariah, Joshua, the high priest of Israel, is depicted standing before the angel of the LORD, but unfortunately he is not alone. Standing faithfully at his right side is the accuser himself, Satan. Revelation 12:10 also describes Satan as *the accuser of our brothers and sisters who accuses them before God day and night.* What profound insight into the reality of our struggles! If Satan's occupation is to stand before God day and night bringing accusations against us, we are very likely to feel the effects of such constant badgering. But if we look further into this astounding vision given to Zechariah, we see the Lord's response to such accusations. *The LORD said to Satan, 'The LORD rebuke you, Satan! The LORD, who has chosen Jerusalem, rebuke you'...Now Joshua was dressed in filthy clothes as he stood before the angel. The angel said to those who were standing before him, 'Take off his filthy clothes.' Then he said to Joshua, 'See, I have taken away your sin, and I will put rich garments on you'* (Zech 3:2-4). Oh, see how our Advocate comes to our defense against Satan's accusations! In addition to His defending us, He also exchanges our garment of sin and shame for a rich, new garment of purity and righteousness. Although, even after being clothed with the righteousness of Christ, Satan will still bring false accusations against us until his ultimate destruction. Yet our only defeat is if we choose to believe his lies instead of God's truth. Therefore, let us arm ourselves with every spiritual weapon afforded in Christ! In Jesus, we stand blameless and victorious in the sight of God. *They triumphed over him (Satan) by the blood of the Lamb and the word of their testimony (Rev 12:11).*

I know he's standing right beside me,
His aim to accuse, not to let me go free.
He wants to destroy me, to steal my joy,
To make me believe his devilish ploys.
Though standing before You, I need not hide,
Even if he is still standing right to my side.
In the light of Your glory, tender eyes I see,
Of the One who has clothed me in all purity.
Now the voice that I hear still nagging beside,
Says nothing of truth and only vents lies.
So accuse no more, I won't listen to you,
For my Father rebukes you, and I do too!

Day 54
Prayer and Thanksgiving

Do not be anxious about anything, but in every situation, by prayer and petition, with thanksgiving, present your requests to God...He did not waver through unbelief regarding the promise of God , but was strengthened in his faith and gave glory to God, being fully persuaded that God had power to do what He had promised. Philippians 4:6, Romans 4:20-21.

What a challenge it is for us today to not waver in unbelief! Often our wavering is in the waiting. We could have maybe stood firm if our request had been granted as quickly as it were spoken, but rarely is that the case. Our faith is greatly burdened in the seasons of silent waiting. But alas! There is a daily prescription for the symptoms of a stressed faith in waiting. And that sure remedy, my sweet friend, is prayer and thanksgiving! Our every anxious thought ought to be replaced with the petitions of a child who is eagerly expectant of his or her Father's response. And do these prayers have to be offered with a dry eye and encouraged heart? Absolutely not! They are to be offered with a genuinely sincere and humble heart to the One who sees and knows our inmost thoughts. They are to be offered as worship in spirit and the truth of God's sovereign control over all things. They are to be offered in faith and full transparency, not with unreliable feelings and emotions. Then and only then, according to our faith, will our requests be granted to us (Matthew 9:29b).

Faith! Stay strong, though the way is dark.
Though the tide's come in,
Though we've missed the mark!

Faith! Don't waver when temptations speak,
When our flesh is frail and our hearts are weak.

Faith! Keep looking to the Master's hand,
Keep waiting on Him,
Keep trusting His plan!

Day 55
On Guard

They would spend the night stationed around the House of God, because they had to guard it; and they had charge of the key for opening it each morning. 1 Chronicles 9:27

Lord, make me a servant,
In Your Temple on high!
This position, I can't earn it,
Though dedicatedly, I'll try!
I'll spend each night there stationed,
Near the door of Your great Throne.
And I'll wait in expectation,
Till the dawning's light is shone.
I'll guard all You've entrusted,
I'll guard it with my life.
In holiness, Thou exalted,
May I reflect all that's inside.
Through faith and true repentance,
You've given me the key.
My sin no longer a hindrance,
The door of salvation, opened to me.
Alert, watching, and waiting,
Outside the Temple gates.
Anxious tendencies restraining,
Beholding Your glory is my fate!

Day 56
Pure Worship

They stood where they were and read from the Book of the Law of the LORD their God for a quarter of the day and spent another quarter in confession and in worshipping the LORD their God. Nehemiah 9:3

Such was the daily agenda for a people desperate to return to their God. Amidst our busy days, weeks, even years, do we set aside time to be utterly stripped of our own contrivances, so that we may allow the Spirit to purify our hearts for worship? How essential this is to hearing from God! The simplicity of such purification is that it can be done right where we stand. We do not have to adapt to a monk's lifestyle to spend time in the presence of Glory. Nevertheless, there is no other way to truly know the heart of God unless we slow our hurried pace and set aside portions of our days to cleanse our souls with Scripture and confession. The more consistent our time spent on such things, the more we will experience His supernatural rest and peace. Consequently, our worship will take on a Heavenly scent that will be received in the very throne room of the King. Thus when He calls us home, we will have already rehearsed with the great assembly of saints, who have reserved for us a seat in the Tabernacle of Zion!

Lord, grant us wisdom, to interpret Your Holy Word,
Humble us to confession, granting every grievance heard.
Purify our worship, make it a reflection of Your grace,

Let us enjoy sweet fellowship, as You meet us in this place.

Day 57
Tailored Trust

O LORD Almighty, blessed is the one who trusts in You.
Psalm 85:12

Lord, help me to trust You even more,
My flesh is so frail, so weak.
Lord, help me to trust You even more,
For I don't feel I have the strength.

Lord, teach me to trust You even more,
My worries, they burden me.
Lord, teach me to trust You even more,
For temptations abound, indeed.

Lord, remind me to trust You even more,
My disappointments are frightening.
Lord, remind me to trust You even more,
For the past is still threatening.

Lord, break me in order to trust You more,
My heart sees this the only way.
Lord, break me in order to trust You more,
For when broken, close to You I stay.

Day 58
Highway to Zion

How blessed is the man whose strength is in You, in whose heart are the highways to Zion! Passing through the valley of Baca they make it a spring; the early rain also covers it with blessings. They go from strength to strength, every one of them appears before God in Zion. Psalm 84:5-7, NASB

Oh, the pilgrimage of God's saints! Those whose hearts are inlaid with the very highways to Zion! What a glorious housing within the soul of the one whose strength is in the Lord. Notice that those whose hearts are set on pilgrimage to Zion must first pass through the valley of Baca. This is a valley of weeping, a valley of sorrow and sadness. Although it is often a dry valley, those saints who pass through make it a spring of tears, softening the hard ground for the next set of weary travelers who are sure to meet its barrenness. The early rain, or the dew of Heaven, accompanies the steps of the pilgrim saint, covering the path with blessings. And yet, does traveling through such valleys leave saintly souls forever tired and weary? On the contrary, they go from strength to strength. For there is no valley in which God does not provide an abundance of grace, which is continually supplied in order to reach the pilgrim's final destination. And what a destination it is! For every one of them appears before God in Zion!

Such is the travel of the weary saint,
Through the valley of Baca with tear stained feet.
Such is the travel of the joyous saint,

On the same path they go from strength to strength!

Such is the travel of the weary saint,
What a dry, desert land they trod.
Such is the travel of the joyous saint,
Early rains turn the hard dirt to sod!

Such is the travel of the weary saint,
The path often they cannot see.
Such is the travel of the joyous saint,
In their heart, the road to eternity!

Day 59

Darkness and Light

If I say, "Surely the darkness will overwhelm me, and the light around me will be night." Even the darkness is not dark to You, and the night is as bright as the day. Darkness and light are alike to You. Psalm 139:11-12

This verse ought to bring overwhelming comfort to those of us who may find ourselves in an overwhelming state! For if we truly believe that God governs both the day and the night, surely He must also govern both our good and bad circumstances. Firm faith is lived in communion and consistency to Jesus Christ. No matter what edge of uncertainty we are brought to, our faith must rely upon the God who stands beside us and the God who also stands below us. Even when we come to taste the finality of death, still our Savior holds possession of our souls and will not hand us over to utter darkness. Therefore our hearts and minds ought to rest as we take advantage of the undeniable privilege of spending each day with our steadfast companion, Jesus Christ.

With a faith not yet sight, to this prayer I will hold,
And though my state may thus confound,
Lord, let Thy truth be told.
I will refrain from all flights of my inconsistencies,
And I will humbly still remember that My God is for me.
Since I do not know tomorrow's course, the changes it may bring,
One day at a time, to You alone, this song I sing:

"Your love is like a fountain, effervescently renewed,
So with joy and delight, I will spend this day with You!
As the sun breaks the morning, there is light to my eyes,
And as the night gently closes, still You steady every sky.
As Your glory fills the heavens, so elates my longing heart,
And Your Word still sustaining, as its truth drives out the dark.
So with seasons, constant changes, my heart shall cling to Thee,
And by truth never failing, always faithful You are to me.
See the night cannot cover, Lord, Your Glory, oh so bright,
For even light and darkness, Lord, to You, are alike."

Day 60
Wake Up!

Wake up! Strengthen what remains and is about to die, for I have found your deeds unfinished in the sight of my God. Remember, therefore, what you have received and heard; hold it fast, and repent. But if you do not wake up, I will come like a thief, and you will not know at what time I will come to you. Revelation 3:2-4

Oh Father, let us not regress,
But continue to earnestly profess,
The fire that burns deep within,
For a holy devotion and repentance of sin!
That the Church would begin to seek Your face,
And anticipate Heaven's full embrace!
That our hearts united, would give our all,
As we eagerly await the trumpet call!
That we'd set aside our wayward goals,
And to Your Word and prayer we'd go!
Seeking that only Your will be done,
And for all people, salvation won!

Day 61
Captured

Therefore I am now going to allure her; I will lead her into the wilderness and speak tenderly to her. Hosea 2:14

When heavy my heart, still these burdens wane,
When Your still small voice soothes all the pain.
When captured in communion sweet,
I can only envision myself at Your feet.
When all my affections are turned to You,
Your still small voice speaks a tender tune.
When surrounded by Your presence above,
I can only hear sweet words of love.
When all I am is Yours alone,
Your still small voice speaks from its throne.
I can only make very few requests known,
Since I am more amazed at how You speak to Your own!

Day 62
Crowns

They lay their crowns before the throne... Revelation 4:10

Oh Father! Let us be rich toward You!
Rich in everything we do!
Give to the poor with open hands,
To show them Christ, as love demands.
To sacrifice our selfish gain,
That only faith and love remain.
To know that You take care of us,
And we can give You all our trust.
For we take nothing of this Home,
Since our treasure lies before Your throne!

Day 63
Waiting on the Lord

Then He said to his disciples, "The harvest is plentiful but the workers are few..." Matthew 9:37

Oh dear heart, what little you know,
Of the One who graciously loves you so.
How anxious you are for the comforts of earth,
Yet how many souls are in need of new birth!
And for these children, your heart is crushed,
Yet all too often the message is hushed.
For why can't you see these fields so ripe?
And why can't you work, tho' there be toil and strife?
But you see, dear heart, you must be trained,
To work the fields, which His blood hath stained.
So set out, you do, with a plan all our own,
But which field to go, you've yet been shown.
Yes, dear heart, the workers are few,
But that's because they don't know what to do.
So return you must to the Master's hand,
So that He alone can show you His plan.

Day 64

Your Name

Those who know Your name trust in You, for You, Lord, have never forsaken those who seek You. Psalm 9:10

Once barely whispered, these names of the Lord,
For holiness and reverence each meaning does afford.

Lord God Almighty, You are the El Shaddai,
You are Jehovah Jirah, The Lord who will provide.

You are the Lord, who is my Shepherd, Jehovah-Raah,
And the Lord who is always there, Jehovah Shammah.

Jehovah Mekoddishkem, the Lord who sanctifies,
El Elyon, You are the God Most High.

El Olam, You are the Everlasting God.
Jealous in Your love for us, this names You, Qanna.

The Lord is our blessed peace, Jehovah Shalom,
The Lord of all the heavenly hosts, Jehovah Sabaoth.

Jehovah Nissi, the Lord my banner, raise it high,
Lord and Master over all of life, You are the Adonai.

The Lord He is our righteousness, Jehovah Tsidkenu,
Elohim and Yahweh, God and Lord of all we do.

He is Jehovah Rapha, the Lord that heals His own,
With His Son, He did complete this...
When He stepped down from the throne.

Yes, many other names may describe our Sovereign King,
But truly, my dear friend, O how wonderful are these!

Therefore...

May we ponder all He is for us and the promises we've received!

Day 65
Hang On Tight

...all the people hung on His words. Luke 19:48

If we were asked to measure our desperation for Christ and all the things of God, how would we rate? For unless we have an insatiable desire for God and His Word, neither will hold our attention. Notice how in the verse, *all the people hung on His words*! How captivating must have been the very words spoken from the lips of Jesus to a crowd desperate for salvation! When we read God's Word, do we cling to it with a firm, two-handed grip, or do we simply read it, never really grasping it at all? Oh beloved, every word and every promise can uphold the full weight of our lives and the circumstances therein. It may be that we are merely trying to hold onto God's Word with one hand, while trying to hold onto our lives with the other. You can rest assured that if you place both hands on the Lord and every promise written in His precious Word, He will, in turn, hold onto you and everything in your life. Trusting Him requires our full embrace!

Your Word never fails to speak,
To my life's greatest needs.
Even when my flesh is weak,
It's on Your truth, my spirit feeds.

I'll hang on tight, to Your word,
To Your promises, I will cling.

I'll submit to all my heart has heard,
And to You, a new song I'll sing!

Day 66
The Rock

When my heart is overwhelmed, lead me to the Rock that is higher than I. Psalm 61:2

Lead me to the Rock,
When my soul is overwhelmed,
When my heart and flesh, they fail me,
When winds break loose the helm.
And every torrent of great trial,
Seems to beat upon my sails,
Surely these storms will overtake me,
These raging waters will prevail!
My cries are panic stricken,
And my emotions, as the sea,
Which tosses its afflicted,
Its victims lent to weakening.
And at the point of near surrender,
At the brink of giving in,
When no fight is left within me,
The tempest looks to win.
Yet it is there, beyond the shadow,
The thick blanket of the night,
I see but a mere flicker,
I see a flashing light!
And beneath its brilliant calling,
It stands bright, above the sea,
Firmly planted, never moving,
Upon the Rock, it's calling me!
So I fix my compass firmly,
Setting sails now once again,
Revived, renewed to seek safe landing,
On the Rock, where I can stand!

Day 67

Perfectly Patient

Surely the arm of the Lord is not too short to save, nor His ear too dull to hear. Isaiah 59:1

Oh Lord, is there anything You can't do?
The earth is all Your own!
Oh Lord, is there anything too hard for You?
Your mercy breaks the dawn!

Oh Lord, is there anything too far gone,
For Your mighty arm to reach?
Oh Lord, is there anything withheld too long,
That Your Spirit a lesson can't teach?

Oh Lord, is there anyone You can't heal?
Your power can raise the dead!
Oh Lord, is there anyone Your Spirit can't seal?
For even the vilest bows his head!

Oh Lord, is there anyone You can't save?
So patient You are with all!
Oh Lord, is there anyone who would be brave,
Enough to trust the Master's call?

Day 68
The Fourth Watch

He saw the disciples straining at the oars, because the wind was against them. About the fourth watch of the night He went out to them, walking on the lake... Mark 6:48

What difficulty in your life has you straining at the oars? Does it seem as though the wind is against you, making it even more difficult to fight the raging waters? If so, then what great comfort you can take in our text today as we read that, He (Jesus), saw the disciples straining at the oars. Jesus can see your struggle, my dear friend. In fact, He is watching, while standing on the shore and merely waiting until the fourth watch of the night to meet you again. From evening until the fourth watch, between the hours of three and six in the morning, Jesus kept His eye on His disciples. He knew their boat would not sink and He knew that even though the winds were against them, the storm would not overtake them. It may seem that Jesus is nowhere near you to calm the storm you are rowing in. But take courage, He is standing on solid ground, keeping His watchful eye on you and allowing your faith to be strengthened. Do not be discouraged, He will not stand far off for too long. He is waiting until the faintest break of dawn to walk out on those same waters of affliction and rejoin you in the boat.

These waters that I'm rowing in, I feel are drowning me!
I strain at the oars, but to no avail, I'm still blown out to sea!

Captain, You've abandoned ship! Oh, why won't You
return?
Can't You see, the wind and waves? For rest, my body
yearns.
Captain, please! I don't understand? Won't You
rescue me from the storm?
Look, the boat! It's breaking now and its sails will
soon be torn!
Dear sailor, I can see the storm, it's right in front of
Me.
I see the waves, the wind, the rain, the threatening of
the sea.
I have kept My watchful eye on you, from evening
until now,
And know the strain has wearied you, but it's what I
have allowed.
It's hard for you to understand, how I choose to test
your faith,
But unless the boat is rocked a bit, a heart won't
reveal its sway.
For I need you to be anchored, knowing My presence
is always near,
And I need you to know I'm watching, there is no need
to fear.
So wait a little longer, therefore, continue in the
strain,
At dawn I'll walk right out to you, and My peace I'll
bring again.

Day 69
Moving Mountains

I will give them an undivided heart and put a new spirit in them; I will remove from them their heart of stone and give them a heart of flesh. Ezekiel 11:19

If I had faith to move mountains,
What would that really mean?
For why would the mountains need to move,
And even so, is such a sight ever seen?
But, ah, dear one, you see now,
The mountains are Mine to move,
And though you cannot see how,
Where I take them, your faith will prove!
Since faith comes through hearing,
And hearing through My Word;
If your faith's in need of rearing,
This I'll accomplish, rest assured.
But something we must settle,
Is it your will or it is Mine?
For it's faith that fights the battle,
And through victory, My Spirit shines!
See, I only need a vessel,
Broken into trust.
And I want someone to wrestle,
Through prayer, this is a must.
So what it all comes down to,
Seek, then ask, then knock.
And all My power will work through—
A faith more solid than rock.
So when a mountain's in need of moving,
You can rest secure.
And know that it's My doing,

Though the outcome seems obscure.
For there's mountains all around you,
They cover a sinner's heart.
And My will is to send My truth—
To make the hardness split apart.
My Spirit moves a mountain,
Every single day.
When one sinner drinks of the fountain,
And in their heart, salvation remains!

Day 70
Simple Faith

And without faith it is impossible to please God... Hebrews 11:6

Oh, the simplicity of faith verses the complexity of fear! So much of our anxiety comes from our not knowing the outcome of our distressing situations. We think that if we only lived with an abundance of our earthly needs continuously being met, then we could rest from our worries and live peacefully. Or if a situation would only work out exactly to our liking, then we could set it aside. But our faith in this life is not merely a means to an end. We are not to simply hold our breath and only hope that God will work all things together for our good. Rather, we are to know and believe that God will work all things together for our good, despite our idea of what the outcome should or should not be. For in all things, our ultimate goal ought to be that we please Him. Our faith is formed by a genuine and sincere relational trust. Our faith is also strengthened by a calm and steadfast trust. This is the kind of faith which allows us to love Christ so much, that we ought to feel guilty for allowing fear to overcome us and take the place of our dependency upon God. We can only please Him and we can only truly rest in Him when we are certain that God is for us and not against us. And when we whole-heartedly believe that His plan, no matter how unsure things may seem, is perfect, then we can trust Him with everything. *Let the simplicity of faith triumph over your fears today and pray that no matter what your need, the Master will have His way.*

Weakened faith, that's all that seems—
To be what I possess.
Weakened faith, not sure of things,
Or how they'll turn out best.
I stress and worry, "How, oh Lord?"
These things I seem to ask,
"Will You?" "Won't You?" "Can You, Lord?"
"Have I brought too large a task?"
Though knowing You, I can't deny,
Everything You are.
For it's on You alone, I can rely,
Knowing we've come this far.
So what I've now resolved to—
Is quite a simple faith.
One that trusts You to do,
What You've already set in place.
And even if I'm unsure,
Of what You'd have me pray.
Your promises will only insure,
You'll give me what I need this day.
For I only want to please You,
So, Lord, increase my faith!
And I only want to love You,
More than anything, this I pray!

Day 71
Morning Star

He heals the broken hearted and binds up their wounds. He determines the number of the stars and calls each of them by name. Psalm 147:3-4

Can the God of all the universe,
Heal my broken heart?
God of lands, the waters immerse,
Bind what has been torn apart?

Can the One who numbers all the stars,
Calling each by name;
Be the One to remove the bars,
That have bound me behind my shame?

Can the God of every living thing,
Love me as His own?
Can He over me, dance and sing,
While I'm sitting here, crying alone?

Can I dare to think of my heart so bright,
Like a star, can it truly shine?
Can the Master hold out His light,
Over the stars and this heart of mine?

And if He knows each star by name,
Am I not just as favored as these?
Shining in the darkest of night, canst the same,
Be said of me?

So when I question His power to heal,
I have to wait and believe,

That soon the passing clouds will reveal—
The Morning Star living in me!

Day 72

Near You, Jesus

*She had a sister called Mary who sat at the Lord's feet
listening to what He said. Mary has chosen what is better and
it will not be taken away from her.* Luke 10:39, 42

Mary, dear sweet Mary, what kept You at His feet?
Why did you stay, listen all day, and sometimes even
weep?

Mary, dear sweet Mary, what drew you to Him so?
Why did you sit so very still, with nowhere else to go?

Mary, dearest Mary, what did He have to say?
Why did you at His face so gaze, and never look
away?

Mary, sister Mary, please tell me all I ask?
Why did you take this posture over any other task?

Martha, dear sweet Martha, what kept you away?
Why did you not hear His words, and all He had to
say?

Martha, dearest Martha, you've always been so
strong,
But as for me, my greatest need, not met is surely
wrong.

Martha, dearest sister, now come, please, sit with me,
Everything your heart desires, is met here at His feet.

For when all you want is Jesus, nothing else will do.

And no one else can free us; I know you want that too.

So sit here, right beside me; that is all He asks,
He will give us quiet rest, from all our busy tasks.

He'll fill us to overflowing, with a love so sweet,
And leave us ever wanting, just to sit here at His feet.

Day 73

Faith

...According to your faith let it be done to you.
Matthew 9:29b

Faith! Stay strong, though the way is dark.
Though the tide's come in,
Though we've missed the mark!

Faith! Don't waver when temptations speak,
When our flesh is frail and our hearts are weak.

Faith! Keep looking to the Master's hand,
Keep waiting on Him,
Keep trusting His plan!

Day 74
Heavenly Respite

In peace I will lie down and sleep, for You alone, Lord, make me dwell in safety. Psalm 4:8

When we truly rest in the Lord, our soul delights in the richest of fare. Completely resting our body, mind, and soul requires a release of everything that is weighing so heavily upon us. Even if it is only for a brief time, while lying upon our beds, we are invited, by the Spirit to lay our burdens down. To lie down and sleep in peace, knowing our lives are kept safe by the One who holds them in the very palm of His hand. We can rest, also, in knowing that the lives of those whom we love do not go unnoticed, nor do our prayers for them go unanswered. And even those things, which encumber our daily routines, can be handed over and themselves be put to sleep for a while. Therefore, when we experience this kind of burden—releasing rest, we are able to receive the new mercies awaiting us in the morning. These are the new mercies, promised by our Father, which we can directly apply to our various trials, that we will inevitably face in the coming day. *Lord, please allow us a Heavenly respite, as we lay our heads down this very night!*

Tis better still to rest awhile,
To wait upon thy bed.
To silence all the mind doth rile,
And feel repose instead.

Tis better to release thy quest,

To His sovereign care.
To give thy body somber rest,
And receive thy tranquil fare.

Day 75
Quiet Strength

...in quietness and in confidence shall be your strength...
Isaiah 30:15

Lord, help us to always think things through,
Listen before we speak.
Let the quietness which summons You,
Turn our weakness into strength.

Help us train our lips for silence,
Let our countenance be true.
In all things, seeking balance,
Block not Your Spirit, flowing through.

Let our lives be lived in confidence,
Though seeking not to be held high,
May our quietness offer no defense,
And You alone, be glorified!

Day 76
The Real Struggle

Put on the full armor of God, so that you can take your stand against the devil's schemes. For our struggle is not against flesh and blood.. Ephesians 6:11-12

What a great reminder, in the midst of our daily struggles, that we are not fighting against flesh and blood, but against the devil's schemes! This reality takes things up a notch as we begin to see more clearly the deceptive lies of Satan. Whether our battle surfaces through difficult relationships, circumstantial defeat, or even severe temptations, we can see that what we are fighting is so much more than these. And if our struggle is so much more than these, then the only way to understand the enemy's tactics is to line every distressing encounter up with God's ultimate plan and purpose. Stepping back and gaining an eternal perspective with the aid of the Holy Spirit and the foundation of God's Word, gives us the field advantage. Not only will we possess the field advantage, but we will also be privileged to see the raging battle from an arterial standpoint. And when we do, we can look beyond the hills and see God's armies advancing!

I have this calling, You have portioned to me,
Please help me, Lord, use it appropriately!
Strengthen my heart, rid me of fear,
Help me to realize, You are always near!
Fill me with oil, to keep lit the flame,
Remind me in You, I will never be shamed.
Help me to fix all my purposes on You,

Knowing I live for the Faithful and True!
So be brave, be strong, be armed for the task,
For the battle is raging, but His army is vast.
Soon we will see, that the victory is won,
Gaze in the clouds, at the descending Son!
He is working and ready, when the Father says, "Go!"
And even that day, Jesus claims not to know.
So with Him we wait and work with all might,
For salvation imparted, let us "fight, fight, fight!"

Day 77
The Body of Christ

Instead, speaking the truth in love, we will grow to become in every respect the mature body of Him who is the head, that is, Christ. From Him the whole body, joined and held together by every supporting ligament, grows and builds itself up in love, as each part does its work. Ephesians 4:15-16

We all come from different walks, we all have different needs.
We all have hurts we're hiding, and battle insecurities.

We all need an outlet, a loving, listening ear.
We all need someone caring, standing very near.

None of us is perfect, since we walk often in the flesh.
None of us has learned it, since we daily have our tests.

But we all can come together, beating as one heart.
We all can show each other love, to aid the hurting parts.

For Jesus is our Master, the Head from which we flow.
And we'll grow a little faster, working out salvation as we go!

Day 78
Despite the Unknown

Do not be afraid, little flock, for your Father has been pleased to give you the kingdom. Luke 12:32

Uncertain, so uncertain, everything I see;
Uncertain, so uncertain, all around, depravity!

Unknown, so unknown, is the future of this life;
Unknown, so unknown, circumstances wrong or right!

Unsteady, so unsteady, the trials that come my way;
Unsteady, so unsteady, are the details of each day!

Though despite the fog that settles, underneath a starry sky,
And despite all that's unanswered, in such challenging of times;

Certain, I am certain, that my God is for me!
Certain, I am certain, by the Cross He's set me free!

Knowing, I am knowing, that eternity awaits!
Knowing, I am knowing, a glorious outcome is my fate!

Steady, I am steady, on His Word when trials come!
Steady, I am steady, since to the Kingdom I belong!

Day 79
Abba Father!

The Spirit you received does not make you slaves, so that you live in fear again; rather, the Spirit you received brought about your adoption to sonship. And by Him we cry, "Abba, Father." The Spirit Himself testifies with our spirit that we are God's children. Romans 8:15-16

How often we become enslaved by fear when we give ear to Satan's lies! Lies whispering to our spirit, telling us that if we were really children of God, why would He allow such things to take place in our lives? Or if we were really children of God, why has He not come to our aid or answered us favorably in our present circumstances? The enemy's aim is to have us believe that our circumstances dictate our adoption as sons and daughters, by the Spirit we have received. Therefore, if we question who we are in Christ Jesus when severe trials befall us, we will be tempted to question God's genuine love for us as a father and instead, maybe envision Him as a cruel slave master. However, when we pull back the veil of deception, the Holy Spirit once again reveals to us our identity in Christ. It is by this witness of the Spirit, that we have the right, in whatever circumstances we are in, to cry, *"Abba, Father!"* By this confession of who He is to us, we can claim every promise given us by Him in His Word! So when there is doubt in our hearts concerning our inheritance as children of God, the Spirit removes the uncertainty by testifying to the truth. By His testimony, we can stand, we can rejoice, and we can press on, not because of what we are experiencing in this life, but because of who God is and who we are in Christ!

We cry, "Abba Father!" Not by circumstances seen.
We cry, "Abba Father!" Through a blood—bought victory!

We cry, "Abba Father!" Bowing as His humble child.
We cry, "Abba Father!" For us, His passion is unbridled!

We cry, "Abba Father!" In every season of this life.
We cry, "Abba Father!" To Him, morning, noon, and night!

We cry, "Abba Father!" While held safely in His arms.
We cry, "Abba Father!" Till kept in Heaven, from all harm!

He is like a father to us, tender and sympathetic to those who reverence Him. For He knows we are but dust, and that our days are few and brief, like grass, like flowers, blown by the wind and gone forever. Psalm 103:13-15, TLB

Day 80
Where Do We Go?

...He endured the cross, scorning its shame...Hebrews 12:2

Where do we go, when all hope seems lost;
When the wicked succeed and the innocent tossed?

How do we cope, with what we don't understand;
When we know in our hearts, this wasn't His plan?

What do we feel, toward those who despise;
Who hate what is right and to Truth, close their eyes?

How can we pray, when our hearts are in pain;
When we feel left alone, isolated, and shamed?

To the Cross, to the Cross, this is where we must go!
To the emblem of shame, that has ransomed our souls!

To the Cross, to the Cross, this is where we must stay!
To the place where our hearts, can discern all His
ways!

To the Cross, to the Cross, for a life glorified!
For others to know, it's in Christ we abide!

Day 81
Eternal Life

For our light and momentary troubles are achieving for us an eternal glory that far outweighs them all. 2 Corinthians 4:17

Lord, I'm frustrated, beyond all belief!
When will I receive, any sort of relief?
I feel so useless, so angry, so bad,
I have no joy, I am so very sad.
There's so many trials, I don't understand,
Maybe all expectations, have been too grand?
My days are filled, with so many things,
Yet unfulfilled desires, fade like dreams.
How am I to feel, have I got it all wrong?
Did I make a mistake, did I wait too long?
Should I have planned, some alternate life?
One that was easy, with a lot less strife?
Or am I living, the one You planned?
Is it in Your presence, that I still stand?
If the veil was lifted, could I then see,
That this is the life, that's been tailored for me?
That it's all the things, that make me feel bad,
That will one day be used, to make others glad?
That unless I experience, the darkest of days,
I can never understand, all Your infinite ways?
And that I might be shallow, empty, and vain,
Unless I experience, some measure of pain?
Could there yet be a greater, plan in mind,
To make my character, like jasper shine?
So instead of about all my "feelings" obsess,
I should be on my knees and to You confess,
That I desperately need, You now in my life,
To show me the truth and banish the lies!

To show me the frailty, of this earthly life,
And that what really matters, is on eternity's side!
Then unveil my eyes, so that I can see,
The army of angels, surrounding me!
The cloud of witnesses, cheering me on,
The hosts of angels, singing their song!
The Ancient of Days, taking His seat,
The loved ones and friends, I'll soon again meet!
The River of Life, flowing from the Great Throne,
The Tree of Life and the streets of gold!
The table set, for Your beloved bride,
Which one day soon, You will bring to Your side!
Clothed with white and standing in praise,
To glorify You and Your Holy Name!
To bow before, the feet of Christ,
Having received the prize, of eternal life!

Day 82
How Long?

How long, Sovereign Lord... Revelation 6:10

How long, Sovereign Lord, will the enemy prevail?
Snatch lives of the innocent and the living ones assail?
How long, Sovereign Lord, until our sufferings will cease?
We groan in all our brokenness, for Your Kingdom, God of Peace.
How long, Sovereign Lord, until You break the seals?
Trumpets sound, lightings flash, rumbling, thunder peals!
How long, Sovereign Lord, until the wicked fall?
Your saints in Heaven all cry out, on earth, Your children call!
How long, Sovereign Lord, until You separate the chaff?
Wield the scepter, sharpen the sword, hand Moses back his staff?
How long, Sovereign Lord, until the Day is here?
Our lamps are lit, our oil filled, You must be very near!
How long, Sovereign Lord, must the enemy deceive?
A nation set on godlessness, setting demons free.
How long, Sovereign Lord, it's Your face alone, we seek!
Come quickly now to save us, bring Your comfort to the weak!
How long, Sovereign Lord, till You ransom all the lost?
Their debt is paid, their sin atoned, You suffered all the cost!

How long, Sovereign Lord, though it's your healing now we need,
The martyrs, Lord, the victims, hold them close, dear Father, please.
How long, Sovereign Lord, till you return to take us home?
For one day this sin—tainted earth, no longer will we roam!

Day 83
He Knows!

"For I know the plans I have for you," declares the LORD, *"plans to prosper you and not to harm you, plans to give you hope and a future." Jeremiah 29:11*

You may have this verse memorized. I commend you if you do because it means that the answer to all your anxiety about the future, already lies within the very fabric of your soul. Although, within this treasure of truth, I ask you to ponder these two words...*He knows*! What an ocean of comfort, what a reservoir of peace, what a spring of mercy, and what a shower of blessing, are found in these two little words...*He knows*. When we do not know, when we cannot fathom, when we simply do not understand...*He knows*. When the plan seems to be no plan at all...*He knows*. When the future seems devoid of any form of prosperity...*He knows*. And is it Jeremiah telling us that *He knows,* or does the Lord Himself, taking full responsibility for our lives, say, *I know*! "I know the plans I have for you." Beloved, He knows the plans that He has for you. Therefore, even if no one on this earth, including you, knows the plan...*He knows*! Place all your dependency upon Him because today and every day, He knows the plans He has for you.

He knows the plan for my life,
Every step He sees!
Every morning, noon, and night,
He's watching over me!
His plan for me will prosper,

He will not bring me harm!
In me, a trust He'll foster,
Showing deeds of His right arm!
A blessed hope and a future,
Is what He has in store!
Therefore, each day I'll nurture—
This heart to love Him more!

Day 84
Shiloh

The Lord continued to appear at Shiloh, and there He revealed Himself to Samuel through His Word. 1 Samuel 3:21

Imagine lying in the very tabernacle which housed the sacred Ark of the Covenant! Would peace and rest not be companions to your soul if every night your head rested in the presence of the veil shrouding the Mercy Seat? It was there, at the tabernacle, in Shiloh, the "place of rest," where a small boy heard the voice of God. In his eagerness to know the One whose presence filled the Holy of Holies, he inclined his whole being to receive the words spoken of the Lord. And oh, how the Lord was inclined to speak to a heart so tender to the Spirit's calling! "Here I am! Here I am, You called me!" Samuel never questioned that he was the one to whom the Lord was speaking. And if by chance, the Lord had been addressing someone else, I can imagine that Samuel would have nevertheless claimed every word for himself! Oh, that we would have a heart like Samuel! That we would find a place of rest, a Shiloh, in the midst of our busy lives, so that the Living God of all the universe might reveal Himself to us through His Word. Samuel would have loved to possess the Scriptures from Genesis to Revelation and to have heard the testimony of Jesus! To have known that one day, represented on the Mercy Seat, Jesus Christ, the Son of God would shed His precious blood to atone for the sin of all mankind. And as Samuel gazed at the veil, did he know that the finished work of the Cross would tear it from top to bottom in Jerusalem's temple? And that this torn veil would symbolize our Lord, therefore making a way for everyone to commune with the Holy of Holies Himself? Oh beloved, let us not forget that we possess all of Heaven and earth in Christ Jesus. Therefore, find your Shiloh and rest, so that through His Word, the Creator of it all, may be inclined to reveal Himself to you!

Shiloh, Shiloh, a blessed place of rest,
A place of Holy presence,
Where I make my one request.

Speak! Speak! Reveal Yourself to me!
Desperately I seek Your face,
Just once, Lord, let me see!

Shiloh, Shiloh, where I will ever stay,
A place I lay my weary soul,
And commune throughout my day.

Here I am! Here I am! Lord, are you calling me?
While resting in Your presence now,
Your very Word does speak.

Shiloh, Shiloh, no veil shrouding Your grace,
I enter through the curtain,
Where upon the seat, You took my place.

Day 85
No Trials, Please

*In all this you greatly rejoice, though now for a little while
you may have had to suffer grief in all kinds of trials. These
have come so that the proven genuineness of your faith—of
greater worth than gold, which perishes even though refined
by fire—may result in praise, glory and honor when Jesus
Christ is revealed. 1 Peter 1:6-7*

Oh Father, please forgive me,
For I'd rather push trials away;
I'd rather they somewhere else be,
And far off I wish they'd stay!

But these trials, they leave me tokens,
Priceless virtues from above;
Very specific things You've chosen—
For my life, with compassion and love.

These trials You use to sharpen,
My character, my heart, and mind;
And my spirit within doth hearken,
"Please, Holy Spirit, my life, refine!"

So if trials bring me nearer,
To understanding Your infinite grace;
Then I will think it only dearer,
For Your allowing me them to face.

This still does not make them easy,
Yet one day I'll understand;

Until then I'll find joy in needing—
To walk through them with You, hand in Hand.

Day 86

A Glorious Perception

See, I am doing a new thing! Now it springs up; do you not perceive it? I am making a way in the wilderness and streams in the wasteland. Isaiah 43:19

How many distractions come our way, which skew our perception of what God is doing in our lives! Or aside from distractions, maybe life has been such an uphill climb for us that we have adopted a pessimistic perception of anything new that comes our way. Disappointment, discouragement, doubt, depression, a downcast spirit, all these have a way of blinding us from the very things that God is working in our lives, for our good. And not only for our good, but for our best! He longs to delight us with His presence and to give us not only life, but abundant life! Life lived to the maximum potential of what He created us to be to glorify Him. However, if we do not perceive it or choose not to perceive what God is doing in our lives, we may miss it. If we try to rationally explain away every nudge, every blessing, every verse given us directly from Scripture—all pointing to the new thing He is bringing about, then we miss it. God, in His graciousness and mercy, may bring it to our attention again in the future, but sadly, some of the fruit that would have accompanied it may, already be spoiled. It's not that He cannot produce more fruit or give us more power from the Spirit on the next go round, but we may very well miss out, due to our initial disobedience in not trusting Him. We must strive to wait patiently, with much anticipation, to see glorious manifestations of His Spirit in our lives and in the lives of others. Oh friend, it may be that we need to give ourselves permission to be excited about the things God is doing in our lives! Because it just might be, that at this very moment, He is *making a way in the wilderness and streams in the wasteland. Do you not perceive it?*

A glorious perception!
Lord, this is what we seek!
A glorious perception
To see Your will complete!

A glorious perception,
Seeing new things springing up!
A glorious perception,
So let us take and drink the cup!

A glorious perception,
To see Your flowing streams!
A glorious perception,
Far beyond our wildest dreams!

Day 87
His Love, His Strength, His Peace

Turn, Lord, and deliver me; save me because of Your unfailing love....Summon Your power, God; show us Your strength, our God, as You have done before...The Lord gives strength to His people; the Lord blesses His people with peace. Psalm 6:4, 68:28, 29:11

We cannot exhaust Your love—
So patiently we wait,
To see descending from above,
Your Hand to guide our way.

We cannot exhaust Your strength—
So empty we will stay,
To wait or go whatever length,
Your Word we will obey.

We cannot exhaust Your peace—
So full our hearts remain,
To know our burdens we can release,
Your Spirit will always sustain.

Day 88
The Cross Awaits

When it was almost time for the Jewish Passover, many went up from the country to Jerusalem for their ceremonial cleansing before the Passover. John 11:55

Lord, we come up to Jerusalem,
To cleanse our hearts and minds,
And in Your presence, receive mercy,
Make us a living sacrifice.

The standard set before us,
You are the spotless Lamb.
Without stain, without blemish,
Rejected Stone, the Great I AM!

The time had come for You to enter,
Yet Your city, held no throne.
Every foe You could have conquered,
Yet You chose to die alone .

So purify our hearts, Lord,
As we confess our grievous sins.
Near the Temple may we walk toward,
The washing bowls, the Great Basin.

Kneeling there, beside the waters,
We must wash our hands and feet.
As we gather with the others,
All professing self-defeat.

In preparation for the Passion,
May we enter through the gates.

Pondering in humble fashion,
The Cross for us, daily awaits.

Day 89

Passover Preparation

Now the Passover and the Feast of Unleavened Bread were only two days away...While He was in Bethany, reclining at the table...Mary took about a pint of pure nard, an expensive perfume; she poured it on Jesus' feet and wiped His feet with her hair. She broke the jar and poured the perfume on His head. "She has done a beautiful thing to Me. She poured perfume on My body beforehand to prepare for My burial."
Mark 14:1, 3, 6, 8, and John 12:3

Oh Mary, had you any thought,
Of what this act did mean?
The precious items that you bought,
Prepared the body of a King!

From a broken heart of gratitude,
The fragrant oil flowed.
With the humblest of attitude,
You gave your all, to Him alone.

Kneeling there, beside His feet,
Soon to be pieced and bruised.
Jesus reclining in His seat,
The others skeptically amused.

As you poured the nard, the perfume,
You gathered up your hair,
Disturbed by nothing in the room,
You wiped His feet with care.

Then rising slowly to your feet,

You kindly made your way,
At His brow, His eyes you meet,
And He whispered, "It's okay."

By Your Savior's confirmation,
You broke the costly case.
His eyes closed in affirmation,
"It's here a crown of thorns, they'll place."

Then a prayer He whispered softly,
To His Father up above.
"Prepare this table now before Me,
Conquer My enemies with love."

And as He lay there still reclining,
Only Jesus really knew,
This blessed act, divine in timing,
Prepared His body for the tomb.

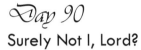

Day 90
Surely Not I, Lord?

"Surely not I, Lord? Even if all fall away on account of You, I never will. Even if I have to die with You, I will never disown You." Matthew 26: 22, 33, 35

We walked by Your side, both day and night,
The miracles, the power, You revealed in our sight,
When You said, "Come, follow" our souls took flight!
Surely not I, Lord? Surely, not I?

Yes, even if all were to fall away,
Surely, dear Rabbi, we would stay!
We can go with You now, yes we can pray!
Surely not I, Lord? Surely, not I?

If we must die, let it be as You say,
We will stand by Your side, we will not run away,
And we will be faithful, from night until day!
Surely not I, Lord? Surely, not I?

Yet, we failed You, Lord, we fell away,
We denied You and left You and went astray,
And we hung our heads in utter shame!
Surely we tried, Lord? Surely, we tried?

As You hung, on that tree, You writhed in pain,
Your blood was upon us, it left its stain,
And we swore our faith would never remain!
Surely we tried, Lord? Surely, we tried?

But to our surprise, You rose from the grave,
You conquered death, when Your body, You gave,

And from eternal damnation, our souls, You saved!
Surely, You are alive, Lord! You are alive!

Your grace, Your mercy, the forgiveness of sin,
In our condemned condition, we could never win,
But You've brought all Your sheep back into the pen,
Yes, You are alive, Lord! YOU ARE ALIVE!

Day 91
This Hour

...But this is your hour, when darkness reigns. Luke 22:53

This was your hour, you wicked Pharisees;
When darkness gave power and you bowed your
knees.

This was your hour, a short one indeed;
When played like a puppet, to fulfill Satan's scheme.

This was your hour, when darkness reigned;
When the forces of evil, brought all to shame.

This was your hour, set to slay the Lamb;
To tear His body and pierce His hands.

This was your hour, yet prophecy fulfilled;
Since if not for this hour, we'd never be healed!

This was your hour, but praise God, no more!
For death no longer keeps us, out of Heaven's open
door!

Day 92
My Name, His Hands

See, I have engraved you on the palms of My hands... Isaiah 49:16

One day we will see it! One day we will gaze upon the palms which voluntarily opened so that our name could be, not merely written, but engraved on the hands of our Savior. The soft tissue was penetrated and pierced so that our lives could be forever held in the grip of His love. And by this eternal wound, our sins are swept away and our souls raptured by His infinite grace! *...by His wounds, you have been healed (1 Peter 2:24b).*

Open Your hand that I may see,
The picture You have engraved of me.

Why did You choose to inscribe it this way,
Why did it happen on such a dark, dreadful day?

Instead of a pen, a rusty nail made this sketch,
Instead of ink, it was blood that was etched.

Open Your hand that I may see,
The picture You have engraved of me.

Day 93
The Weight of Sin

The earth shook, the rocks split... Matthew 27:51b

The weight of sin,
Wrapped like a cloak,
Round the shoulders of this Man.
The weight of sin,
Never taken off,
Held on by Love's demand.

The weight of sin,
His body pulled,
From Heaven down to earth.
The weight of sin,
His life given to death,
Even from His birth.

The weight of sin,
So heavy, the rocks split,
And the earth did quake.
The weight of sin,
So heavy, the heart of the Father,
Violently ached.

The weight of sin,
Should I carry,
Never could my body uphold.
The weight of sin,
For my freedom,
One day seeing His glory unfold!

Day 94

Conquering King

When you were dead in your sins and in the uncircumcision of your flesh, God made you alive with Christ. He forgave us all our sins, having canceled the charge of our legal indebtedness, which stood against us and condemned us; He has taken it away, nailing it to the Cross. And having disarmed the powers and authorities, He made a public spectacle of them, triumphing over them by the Cross. Colossians 2:13-16

A death that gave us life! Our sin, our legal indebtedness, the dark powers of the spiritual realm, and the dark powers of the earthly authorities, all stood in great opposition to us. But now, having triumphed over all of these by the Cross, our sin...*forgiven*. The charges brought forth from our legal indebtedness ...*canceled*. The reigning dark powers of the spiritual and earthly realms ...*disarmed*. The enemies of God, in hell and on earth, who had mocked the precious Son of God were torn from their pedestals of pride and made a public spectacle! Christ and His glorious, triumphant resurrection restored the Kingdom of God to the ends of heaven and earth and placed the true King eternally over *all things* created for Him and by Him!

Oh dear Lord, when I'm a mess,
When the enemy lurks,
And my soul needs rest,
Remind me to call upon Your name,
Get out my sword, confront the shame.

Cling to all I know is true,
Shut out the lies,
Proclaim Your truth!
Lift up my voice in shouts of praise!
And with my hands, to You, I'll raise!
Not be deceived to cower down,
To isolate or feel shut out!
To wallow in all the woes of life,
Thinking I'm the only one with strife!
But stand back up and say, "AMEN!"
My Savior overcomes and wins!
And I need never be ashamed,
For who I am in Jesus Name!
For no matter what threatens me today,
My Jesus, My King, will have His way!
And He will always see me through,
He's on my side, there's nothing He can't do!

Day 95
Afraid Yet Filled

So the women hurried away from the tomb, afraid yet filled with joy and ran to tell His disciples. Suddenly, Jesus met them. "Greetings," He said. They came to Him, clasped His feet and worshiped Him. Matthew 28:8-9

What an unexpected encounter for the women that morning! Upon their waking, their hearts still ached heavily, hoping that the events which had taken place on that dreadful day of crucifixion were perhaps nothing more than a terrible nightmare. In their state of grief—stricken shock, they carried embalming spices to the tomb thinking they would see yet again the marred, disfigured, and pierced body of the One they loved so deeply. And yet, as they approached the tomb, expecting only to be met with death, they were astoundingly greeted with eternal life! We can only imagine the jolt of emotions as Scripture tells us the women were "afraid yet filled with joy!" Their Jesus was alive! Nothing else, even their own salvation, mattered to them in light of receiving their first love back from the dead. And as He greeted them, all the discouragement and doubt that had invaded their weary souls vanished as they beheld the face of their Savior once again! His beautiful face and loving eyes reassured them that He had never once forsaken them, even in death! Oh, the depth of His love for us! We can only imagine what it will be like to gaze into the face of Jesus when our time on earth is over. Will we be as the women that glorious resurrection morning and clasp the feet of our Savior in worship? Oh, I pray so!

So afraid, yet filled with joy,
Then Who is this they meet?

It's Jesus! Yes, their Rabboni!
They worship at His feet!

Oh Lord, would You come to us,
As we walk this path of life?

Love arising out of darkness,
Greet us with Your saving light!

And when see Your glory,
May our response then be,

Just as the women in this story,
Compelled to worship at Your feet!

Day 96
Burning Within

They asked each other, "Were not our hearts burning within us while He talked with us on the road and opened the Scriptures to us?" Luke 24:32

Oh, to have been on the road to Emmaus when the risen Christ walked and talked with two of His once close followers! Imagine walking alongside Jesus Himself and not recognizing Him! No doubt these two men were drawn to Jesus as they begged Him to stay with them longer and share a meal. And it was not until they broke bread together, that they realized it was their Lord and then suddenly He disappeared. But before Jesus' identity was revealed and their eyes were opened, Jesus first opened the Scriptures to them. And as these very Scriptures, the Old Testament Scriptures, were opened and explained, the hearts of the two men began burning within them. Then finally, when they communed with Jesus by breaking bread with Him, their eyes were opened. My friend, we simply cannot underestimate the power of the spoken Word of God! The Scriptures ought to burn within our hearts in such a way that when we come into fellowship and communion with our Lord, we can truly see Him for who He is! We can believe that everything He has said and promised us is true. And since we are aided by the power of the Holy Spirit, we can be assured that God will use His Word to convict, correct, challenge and change us. But unless our hearts are fully opened to these penetrating truths, our eyes will not be opened to see Jesus.

Therefore, let every word of Scripture gather within your heart like kindling and oil for the flame of the Spirit, to keep the fire forever burning with a passion to one day see Jesus face to face!

I have walked along a desperate road,
Just as those to Emmaus did go.
I have hung my head in utter defeat,
Wondering why You didn't show.

Then I met You on this desert road,
And we walked a mile or so.
I found Your Presence comforting,
And begged You, "Please don't go."

But until You had me listen,
To things I had not known,
Until You explained the Scripture,
All my heart could do was groan.

Though now my heart's on fire,
Burning deep within;
These words, they bring conviction,
"Lord, I repent of all my sin!"

Now as we sit together,
You across from me,
You break the bread, Your body,
And of Your blood, I take a drink.

Jesus! It's You, Jesus!
It's like I always knew,
But until Your Word burned within me,
I realized not the truth!
Please keep this fire burning,

This passion for Your Word!
And keep me ever yearning,
Until my eyes can see You, Lord!

Day 97

Pushing The Gate

They...came to the iron gate leading to the city. It opened for them by itself and they went through it. Acts 12:10

Dear beloved, tell Me, are you pushing against the gate?
In doing so, let Me tell you, you are making a mistake.

For what you fail to see is... there's an angel by your side.
And what you've failed to notice, is I have placed him as your guide.

For there is no key to unlock it, this gate blocking your way.
And no human arm can jog it, so patiently you must wait.

Do not fret or be worried, no need to trouble your health,
No need to rush or be hurried, for the gate will open itself.

Day 98
Guide Me

You are God my stronghold. Why have You rejected me? Why must I go about mourning, oppressed by the enemy? Send forth Your light and Your truth, let them guide me; let them bring me to Your holy mountain, to the place where You dwell. Then will I go to the altar of God, to God, my joy and my delight... Psalm 43:2-4

God is our stronghold! As His children, we know this to be true, yet even with this knowledge, we are still not immune to the attacks of the enemy. These attacks can hit us when our surrounding circumstances and overall exhaustion have pressed hard into us. Even while having the Truth within our hearts and minds, we can still be brought low enough to the point of feeling rejected by God. As a result of our downcast state, we will often go about mourning, further allowing the enemy to oppress us. Oh, that we could be like the Psalmist and cry out to God to rid us of such malady of soul! Never mind what got us so off track! Our soul's purpose must now be to find our way back to the very dwelling place of God. *Send forth Your light and Your truth, let them guide me...* Let His light and truth guide you back to the holy mountain of God, so that you may then go to the altar and be sacrificed once again, surrendering all to your Savior. Then you will find that it is only there where we are reminded that all our joy and delight is found in God alone! *Then I will go to the altar of God, to God, my joy and my delight!*

Dear soul, do you go on mourning, about your
present state?
Has the enemy heard your grieving, wanting to
participate?
Do you feel strong the oppression, much heavier than
before?
Is it causing such depression, once simple joys you now
ignore?
Beloved! You must cry out! You must voice your
wandering heart!
And swiftly the enemy you must rout, before he tears
your life apart!
You must look unto the Heavens, and plead your noble
right,
As a child among the Kingdom heirs, reclaim a victor's
life!
Pray the Father will send forth His light to illuminate
His truth,
Let the Holy Spirit be your guide, your destination He
will prove!
To the mountain He'll return you, to the place His
glory dwells,
To the altar He will bid you, where joy and delight are
never withheld!

Day 99
The Battle Cry

As long as Moses held up his hands, the Israelites were winning, but whenever he lowered his hands, the Amalekites were winning, [therefore] lift up your hands in the sanctuary and praise the Lord. Exodus 17:9, Psalm 134:2 (brackets mine)

Israel was victorious in battle the day Moses stood atop a hill with both hands raised to the Lord of Hosts! Though the Lord brought the victory, it was Moses' faith that brought the Lord's armies to the battle field. For when Moses lowered his hands, Scripture tells us that the enemy would gain footing and begin to win. What a strange thing for God to allow Moses such demonstrative participation in the fight! And yet we see another battle years later on Israel's timeline where God allowed similar participation. 2 Chronicles 20:22 tells us, "As they [the armies of Judah] began to sing and praise, the Lord set ambushes against the men of Ammon and Moab and Mount Seir, who were invading Judah, and they were defeated." Therefore, by such victories, can we not glean for ourselves that if we raise our hands and our voices to the Lord in praise, the enemy will no longer overtake us? Surely it is nonetheless important for us to relay our silent petitions to the Lord, but what if we found that our full and even demonstrative participation against the attacks of the enemy gave us the field advantage? In Christ Jesus, the victory has already been won, yet until He returns, it is our duty as soldiers enlisted in the Lord's army, to raise not only our voices in praise, but our hearts and hands as well. In doing so, we will find that our continued worship will make us courageous warriors who are never lacking victory in our lives over the enemy!

As Moses stood, with unwavering faith,
Upon the mountaintop that day.
The battle raged on, but with no mistake,
The Lord's armies brought victory their way!

When tired arms began to shake,
The lesson of faith took root.
For the hearts of men began to faint,
And the enemy, their lives, overtook.

Yet as men of Judah, with voices raised,
Brought the ambushes of the Lord,
In faith they began to sing and praise,
Enemies falling to each other's sword!

So when battle around us is raging,
And we cannot gain sure ground,
May we, with worship hands engaging,
Make our battle cry a melodious sound!

Day 100
Run Again

You were running a good race, who cut in on you and kept you from obeying the truth? Galatians 5:7

We can gain clear insight from our verse in Galatians today if our hearts will be open to receive it. Let's read this Scripture as if Paul were speaking directly to us. I believe if the truth of this verse were the reality of our lives, we may very well hang our heads in despair. Though instead of being cut in on by someone, maybe we have been cut in on by something. Maybe we can look back ten, twenty, or even thirty years and remember a time when we ran the race well. Then if we ponder carefully, we may recall that somewhere upon the track of life, we fell away just enough to slight our obedience to Christ. Beloved, obedience is not legalism. True unhindered obedience to our Savior will never produce rigidity in our countenance. Absolute obedience will only serve to soften us, strengthen us, and satisfy us in our relationship to Jesus Christ and to others. If life's failures and frustrations have cut in on us while running the race of faith, then we must confess our sin and pray that God will restore us fully, so that we may finish well. We cannot allow our past, our pain, or our passivity to keep us from obeying God's truth and fully living it out in our daily lives. Remember, my friend, you were running the good race and you can run it again! You may just need a little discipline to get back into shape!

Who or what held you back,

Kept you from the race?
Did something get you off track,
Or noticeably slow your pace?

Are you tired, weak and worn out,
Has life's tempest blown you down?
Do your circumstances cause doubt,
Worries bring with them a frown?

Don't forget, dear Christian,
You were running a good race!
Your life was set on mission,
Your energy was grace!

So shake off dusty running shoes,
Stretch prostrate on the floor,
Confess your sin, you can't lose,
Your heavenly Trainer's at the door!

Obedience will be your focus,
Perseverance a major key,
Motivation will keep you closest,
To the One who has set you free!

Day 101
Safely Secure

He will cover you with His feathers and under His wings you will find refuge; His faithfulness will be your shield and rampart. Psalm 91:4

What a beautiful picture of security! If we would only but envision ourselves running to our Father as He lifts His wing to receive us, then folds it back down, completely covering us, drawing us near to His soft, tender breast. It is there, not only under, but utterly hidden in the shadow of His wing, we find refuge. It is there we find rest and security from the restlessness of worry and the anxiety of life. The Holy Spirit will cover our hearts, our souls, and our minds in Christ Jesus. He will shade us from the scorching heat, and protect us from the vilest storms. Dear friend, do not stand alone amidst the trials and temptations of this life. Seek refuge under His tender wing. And as you seek rest, remember that our God is faithful. His faithfulness is a shield and rampart, which is yet another picture of security. However, instead of a tender wing of protection, now we see a solid defense against the enemy. If we only had the spiritual eyes to see what all God's faithfulness, in His purchasing us by the blood of Christ, is fully protecting us from! There is no truer Keeper of the Soul as the Holy Spirit of God. Do not forget what you possess, dear heart! Do not stand alone! Run under His wing and rest secure knowing that nothing can break through the shield and rampart surrounding the children of the Most High.
Run, My child, come to Me,

Under the shadow of My wing.
Let the feathers cover softly,
All your restless wandering.

You are safest with Me,
There is no need to fear.
All that has you weary,
Will fade as you draw near.

I am your shield and rampart,
My faithfulness will keep.
In repentance bring a pure heart,
For the blessed peace you seek.

Day 102
Preferential Paralysis

Make every effort to live in peace with everyone and to be holy; without holiness no one will see the Lord. Hebrews 12:14

What a challenge is presented before us today! *Make every effort to live in peace with everyone...?* Surely, Lord, You don't mean for us to even make peace with those who insult or bagger us? And by no means can You be using the writer of Hebrews to instruct us to make peace even with those who reject and despise You? Ah, but we know better, don't we, my friends. I think more than our difficulty in keeping the peace with those around us, is our difficulty with our so-called, fleshly right to hold on to our own personal preferences. We may prefer not to associate or not to submit in love to those who do not hold to our same convictions. Although, the preferences or opinions we possess usually have nothing to do with the cause of the gospel of Jesus Christ. Instead, they are usually side issues which drive a wedge in our making every effort to live in peace with everyone. The consequence of our staking claim to our own personal preferences therefore results in what can be called preferential paralysis. This is when our own thoughts, feelings, opinions, or agendas prevent us from moving forward, not only in our intimacy with the Lord, but with others as well. If our sole mission and life's goal is to please God and live in peace with Him, then we ought to gladly scuff off everything that hinders such a worthy and holy cause. Today's verse also enlightens us to another truth of the utmost importance. ...*without holiness no one will see the Lord.* Beloved, let's take inventory today to see where our selfish sin nature has deceived us into thinking we have the right to love only those whom we prefer to love. Let's not let preferential paralysis hold us back from seeking and experiencing the holiness of Jesus Christ in our lives, so that we may clearly reflect His image in the lives of others.

So we make it our goal to please Him, whether we are at home in the body or away from it. 2 Corinthians 5:9

A new command I give you: Love one another. As I have loved you, so you must love one another. John 13:34

Day 103
The Cry of Our Day

And this is my prayer: that your love may abound more and more in knowledge and depth of insight, so that you may be able to discern what is best and may be pure and blameless until the day of Christ, filled with the fruit of righteousness the comes through Jesus Christ—to the glory and praise of God. Philippians 1:9-11

Lord! This is our prayer, the cry of our day,
That those in Your image, would seek Your face!
That love would abound, to the lost and the saved,
And no one would hinder, Your infinite grace!
That no longer would lies, replace the truth,
That those lies be revealed, so none could refute.
That the truth would sink to the depth of our souls,
And insight would change all, from young to old.
That salvation would spring from this dry, thirsty land,
And those lost in darkness, would reach for Your Hand!
That discernment would cause all to live blameless and pure,
Being sure to examine, all the day's behavior.
And living this out with immense urgency,
While counting the cost, though salvation is free.
For Your glory to be revealed, in the day of Christ,
And Your judgment unleashed, justice demanding its price!
So fill us with righteousness, let our fruits be ripe,
And offered to all, with the harvest in sight.
Giving praise and honor and glory to You,
As we offer this prayer, may Your faithfulness prove!

Day 104
Sweet & Satisfying Communion

How sweet are Thy words unto my taste! Yea, sweeter than honey to my mouth! Psalm 119:103, KJV

Discouragement and depression leave a bitter taste; a taste so acidic that it seems best not to partake in anything else, but rather leave such a taste alone and wait until it neutralizes. When these pungent feelings of despair reside within, Satan will try to convince us that the reading of God's Word is merely a pastime or another assignment. Therefore, he will place things in our path to push such an obligation to the bottom of our daily task list. Unknowingly, we may even allow bitterness to be directed toward the guilt we feel since we know we ought to spend time in God's Word. On the other hand, we know the truth of the matter is that the Word of God is the only thing that can instantly neutralize such petulance. Sweeter than honey, is the God-breathed message we possess as the standard of our faith. It is more than just words, it is life, it is nourishment, and it is essential to our truly knowing God. Therefore, take your sour soul to the sweet comb of communion and let the honey soothe your sullenness. For unless we partake with the desire to be relieved of our animosity within, we will never come near to Jesus, to the One in whom there is only peace.

Exactly what I need each day—
Is what Your Spirit breathes.
To touch my heart, along the way,

And all my bindings free.
There is no other greater joy—
Than when You speak to me.
No book, no song, none else I'll toy,
Your Word—it's all I need.
So let the honey slowly draw,
Tis sweet to taste the comb.
That satisfies with ner' a flaw,
And bids my cravings Home.

Day 105
Lost and Found

...I consider everything a loss because of the surpassing worth of knowing Christ Jesus my Lord, for whose sake I have lost all things. Philippians 3:8

Broken! From all my selfish pride,
My heart yields to Christ alone!
Broken! From possessing my own life,
My soul bows before His throne!

Broken! From making my own plans,
My agenda the Kingdom's own!
Broken! From making vain demands,
My course to me, need not be shown!

Broken! From gaining man's fair nod,
My approval seeks only Thee!
Broken! From questioning each lent job,
My steps foreordained for me!

Broken! From desiring anything else,
My portion sets firm boundaries!
Broken! From seeking earthly wealth,
My Father owns all cattle and seas!

Broken! From wasting any more time,
My Saviors laid hold of me!
Broken! From discounting all that is mine,
My spirit sealed for eternity!

Day 106
Abased and Abound

I know both how to be abased, and I know how to abound: everywhere and in all things I am instructed both to be full and to be hungry, both to abound and to suffer need. Philippians 4:12, KJV

Abased and abound, two states in which we are instructed to live, constantly held in tension of each other. The reality of each of these very opposing positions is that we truly would not understand one without the other. We would never grasp the depth of suffering that comes upon those whom we encounter regularly if we ourselves were not allowed to be abased. Likewise, we also would never fully enjoy the elevation of our abundance had we not been afflicted with the plight of abasement through our difficult circumstances. *The Lord sends poverty and wealth; He humbles and He exalts (1 Samuel 2:7).* Yet, the goal of our faith, no matter what the circumstances, is to possess a childlike dependency upon a Father who will be with us in both the highs and lows of life. Whether we are abased or whether we abound, we can know that God is faithful to those who belong to Him. What He has instructed will serve to bring Him glory, only if we see all things as coming from His hand.

Oh, the joy of abundance,
Such a wonderful place to be!
Here with no encumbrance,
My heart feels light and free!

Oh, the weight of abasement,
How long in this dreaded state?
Relief, I'm awaiting your advent,
Though I fear you're running late!

The highs and lows of life, Lord,
Must You lend us both of these?
As a rope intertwined with two cords,
One abundance, the other need.

Though with one and not the other,
The rope would quickly snap.
To use it, none would bother,
Strength, this rope would lack.

So with a wisdom I can't fathom,
Keep strong this rope of life.
There's no trial willed at random,
No stillness without strife.

This tension, I then welcome,
Teach me, Lord, dependency!
To keep despairing seldom,
And as child, cling to Thee!

Day 107
Yes and Amen!

For all the promises of God in Him are Yes, and in Him Amen, to the glory of God through us. 2 Corinthians 1:20

All Your promises come to pass,
Even my life, they will outlast!
For there's never a promise,
That did not prove true,
And never a claim unclaimed by You.
Every hope, every song, each word of life,
My earring ways brought back to right.
When sorrows landed, their full weight upon,
Your words, Your spirit, sang me a new song!
Each soothing whisper only arranged,
My heart's broken pieces back together again.
To think I could have made it this far,
Without Your promises, my soul 'd be marred.
Though instead, I seek only the Healer Divine,
Since I fully believe every promise is mine!

Day 108
Pleasant Perspective

LORD, You have assigned me my portion and my cup; You have made my lot secure. The boundary lines have fallen for me in pleasant places; surely I have a delightful inheritance.
Psalm 16:5-6

Where have your boundary lines fallen, friend,
As your gaze at you life today?
Can you ponder the beginning and the end,
Within these safety lines do you stay?

Have you reached your hand to take the cup,
Each time it's been passed to you?
With every embrace, have you held it up,
And by drinking, did follow through?

Now then the portion you've received,
Does it bring you joy each day?
Do you trust Whom you've believed,
Eager in His will to stay?

Does the inheritance you've been promised,
Serve as an anchor for your soul?
Do you delight in the way of a psalmist,
Eager for His glory to behold?

So why do I ask you these questions, per say?
Is your reply, "Of course I do!"
If you agree to all we've discoursed today,
Then sincerely, I'm glad for you!

Though, beloved, do you truly believe Him?

That in perfection, He's tending to you?
And even when darkness does close in,
He remains for you Faithful and True?

For the portion and cup He's assigned you,
May be a taste both bitter and sweet.
Still His lines you mustn't cross through,
By staying within, He with you, will meet.

Jesus offers a pleasant perspective,
To bring us back if we've veered away,
And of our hearts we must be protective,
That we may rejoice in His goodness all day!

Day 109
Unhindered Hope

Those who hope in Me will not be disappointed. In You they trusted and were not disappointed. Isaiah 49:23, Psalm 22:5

Does this promise bring rest to your soul today, my friend? If it does not, read it again and know that God makes good on all of His promises. What disappoints you today? Who or what has failed you, either now or in the past, and left you with a burden too heavy to bear? There is only One who will not fall short of doing that which He has pledged to accomplish in your life. We will disappoint ourselves and even disappoint others time and again, but God will remain faithful. If there is ever an occasion for us to feel genuinely humbled under the mighty hand of God, it is when all our efforts have failed and we realize that only He can complete the work He has willed for all things, in us and around us. Beloved, Jesus will not disappoint you, fail you, or leave you. So believe Him today to do all that He has the ability to do. And what can He do? *Anything!*

You will not disappoint, Lord!
We can trust in You!
There's nothing You will leave void,
You reclaim and You renew!

You will not fail us, Savior!
We rest in Your embrace!
Do not allow us to waiver,
This accomplish by Your grace!

You will not leave us, Father!
We hold Your steady hand!
Gripping tight, lest we falter,
You will fulfill Your plan!

Day 110
Trust Him Today

Yet God is my King from old, Who works deeds of deliverance in the midst of the earth. Then I thought, 'To this I will appeal: the years of the right hand of the Most High.' Psalm 73:12, 77:10, NASB

Is God your King from old? Has He been King over your life and have you lived in full submission to His authority for many days of your existence? The same King from old is still King today and *works deeds of deliverance in the midst of the earth* and in the midst of your life. If we could only pull back the veil to see the process and plan of deliverance in the midst of our circumstances, then our faith would be made sight! Yet, can we honor God by trusting Him, even when a cloud of thick darkness makes it impossible for us to see anything? Isn't our Savior worthy of our praising Him for His faithfulness throughout the ages? If so, then we can make the Psalmist appeal as if it were our very own, by remembering *the years of the right hand of the Most High.* We can appeal to the strength and sovereignty of His mighty right hand, meditating on His past deliverances and sacrifice, which He gave for the salvation of all humankind. Oh, what great a salvation we have received that is still working today and has the everlasting power to bring liberation, even for the neediest souls in the direst circumstances!

Trust Him today with what you don't understand,
Trust Him today for His Sovereign plan!

Trust Him today remembering deeds of old,
Trust Him today for mighty acts foretold!
Trust Him today and submit to His reign,
Trust Him today He is still the same!
Trust Him today to deliver you, friend,
Trust Him today, His mercy knows no end!

Day 111

Eternal Hearts

...He has also set eternity in the human heart; yet no one can fathom what God has done from beginning to end.
Ecclesiastes 3:11

Why is it so hard to say "goodbye" to those we love after their presence no longer graces the earth? Yes, we miss them terribly, but why are there times when the pain of loss cuts so deep that we feel utterly helpless? The answer: We were never created to taste death! We were never created to be separated to such a degree where earth could no longer see Heaven with the naked eye. Adam and Eve walked in the garden with the Lord and fellowshipped with Him until the fall. How devastating for all humanity, due to sin, to no longer enjoy such satisfying communion! Yet, even from the beginning, God knew what it would take to restore our hearts, setting eternity in them once again so that we could, with a faith not yet sight, possess an unhindered, glorious fellowship with the God of Heaven! We cannot fathom what God has done from beginning to end, nor could we ever fully understand why He would give His all for us to live in sweet rapture with Him for all eternity! Even after His knowing that we could never gain, repay, or live up to the undeserved salvation we receive freely through His precious blood, He still gave His life for us! Beloved, if you know Jesus as your personal Savior, you have eternity, not only set in your heart, but fulfilled! Praise be to God, Who, by His magnificent Sovereignty, sees it all from beginning

to end! Through Christ's death on the cross, the battle
for your soul has been won!

Every single human heart,
He has set on eternity!
And only one thing stands to part,
To remain captive or be set free.
By covenant of precious Blood,
In Spirit's ink, our name we sign.
Salvation's overwhelming flood,
Praise God, eternity is mine!
With Sovereign eyes, He sees it,
From beginning to the end.
So in gratitude, let us be spent,
Exuding His righteousness from within!
For one day, we'll be like Him,
Seeing Glory only now foretold.
The veil becoming even more thin,
As eternal life He to us unfolds!

Day 112
Subtle Spiritual Growth

But grow in grace (undeserved favor, spiritual strength) and recognition and knowledge and understanding of our Lord and Savior Jesus Christ (the Messiah)... 2 Peter 3:18, Amp

We do not grow in toiling,
We do not grow with strain.
We do not grow by foiling,
Our plans, they're empty gain.
We do not mature by acting,
Rehearsing all our parts.
We do not mature in fasting,
Unless we're praying in the dark.

On the contrary...

We grow in still submission,
As we lean upon His breast.
We grow in harsh conditions,
Where our Savior gives us rest.
And we mature in sacred fellowship,
With the One who calls our name.
We mature by truth of ownership,
Trusting His promises are ours to claim!

Day 113
Safety Harbor

...We had sailed slowly for a good many days...since the wind did not permit us to go farther. Acts 27:7

God allows the winds of circumstance to carry us along the seas of life. In His sovereign control over all things, God knows the precise direction each wind will take us. Some winds may cause us to drift at sea, while others take us directly to our desired destination. And while each gust has an intended course, there are some whose assignment is to prevent us from going any farther toward the worthy goals that have been assigned to us. Therefore, the pace of life draws, at times, to almost a near halt. Usually these winds are strong, forceful, and unexpected. We may be tempted to allow these wafts to carry us just for the sake of moving forward, yet with such unpredictability in their nature, we do not know where we might end up! So what are we to do when the force of the airstream threatens to overtake us? The answer: we gradually sail along the shore. The shore, being the proof of God's presence in our lives, remains visible as we sail steadily against strong and violent winds. Our boat does not come out of the water, but rather is kept safe by the closeness of the shore as it continues to move along bit by bit toward its intended destination. Beloved, are the winds of circumstance hitting you? Then seek the shore of the Savior's presence. Accept that you may have to sail at a slower pace, but remember that you will soon experience gentle, favorable breezes again.

Beloved, stop struggling, face the wind!
The sails are torn, in need of a mend!
Now steady the sail, let it carry you straight,
In less than deep waters is where you'll wait.
Leave anchor weighed and above the sand,
Stay near shallow ground, with an eye on the land.
Slow and steady, keep traveling this way,
You may sail slowly, a good many days.
But the winds will change and soon favorably,
We'll again chart your course on the vast, open sea!

Day 114
Daily Encouragement

But encourage one another daily, as long as it is called "Today"... Hebrews 3:13

Let it be said of us, that while living in this earthly shell, we encouraged many to keep the faith! If we ourselves have been given any encouragement from being united with Christ, then we are to in turn, while it is still called "Today," encourage others. Where would we be if God had not placed certain Individuals in our lives to build us up? And should we cease to build up the body of Christ when we feel torn down by our own disheartening circumstances? Truly, it is in times of great discouragement and despair that God allows us the opportunity to shift the focus off ourselves and share the uplifting, life-giving message of eternal hope we possess in Christ! Should this extending of Christ's love through encouragement by the message be limited to a mere weekly or monthly endeavor? On the contrary, *"But encourage one anther daily..."* If we are limited in our interaction with others on a daily basis, may we be obedient to this command through our prayers for the saints and for the lost. In turn, if we are constantly surrounded by others throughout our day, may we take extra care to be a vessel for the Holy Spirit and take every opportunity afforded to share the love of Christ!

I shudder to think where I'd be,
Had not encouragement come my way!
Many seeds of hope planted in me,

Were spoken by others each day.
Thank the Lord for those who whispered,
A silent, sweet prayer in their hearts.
And to my life, oh how it ministered,
Shielding me from the Enemy's darts!
So Lord, give me words of encouragement,
To the many souls that come my way!
Make me a light, even in my discouragement,
As long as it is called, "Today!

Day 115
The Power Struggle

To this end I labor, struggling with all His energy, which so powerfully works in me. Colossians 1:29

Notice how Paul, in our verse for today was struggling and striving in his labor for the Lord. Do you feel the strain, dear friend, as you struggle to accomplish what God has called you to do? It may seem that the vision you long for looks to be a muddled mess and you cannot yet relish in any sense of accomplishment or finality. And quite possibly, accompanied with the never ending struggle, is the lack of energy needed to complete even daily tasks. Oh, how we cannot see the Heavenly agenda which God has laid out for our lives! Only an infinitely wise and all-powerful Creator could take even our most seemingly defeated days and use them for our good. Yet, are we to feel continually weathered by the storm of strain to such an extent that we are left to our own strength to carry out that which God has ordained in any given season of our lives? According to Paul, we too can struggle with all His energy, never lacking the strength which our Lord so readily will supply in our times of need. And this everlasting energy does not merely promise to only help us get by. Better yet, it has the ability to work powerfully and supernaturally through our mortal flesh to accomplish that which God has assigned to us.

No matter what you put your hand to,
He will supply the need.

Working powerfully in and through you,
Begging all your frustrations, "Be free!"
If the strain and struggle propels you,
Let His mercy and grace lead on.
Trust Him now for what He will do,
His energy carrying you all along!

Day 116
Showers We Plead

...I will send down showers in season; there will be showers of blessing. Ezekiel 34:26b

Over the seal of my kitchen window is placed this precious, yet profound promise written on a note card. While meditating and pondering each word of triumphant truth found within this Scripture, two phrases stand out: *showers in season* and *there will be*. If gazed over too quickly, we may miss their significance. However, considering that God sends down *showers in season* helps us to understand why we may have yet to experience the showers of blessing we have prayed and longed for. It helps us to realize that God has not needlessly withheld them from us, as much as He is waiting for the very season of our lives when we will receive those best and need them most. "But we need them now," we may be tempted to say! Although, if we could gage the length and breadth of the seasons of our lives, then maybe we would have a better understanding of what God is doing and why He is choosing to either donate or defer the blessing. And if we settle also on the second phrase, we see the highlight of the promise itself...*there will be*! The promise within the promise is found here in these three little words! Praise God that He tells us there will be showers of blessing! Therefore if we are pleading for a blessing, let us lean with the full weight of our body, mind, and soul upon the promise that there will be showers of blessing in season!

Showers of blessing,
Showers of blessing we need.
Mercy drops round us are falling,
But for the showers we plead!

Showers of Blessing, Hymn
Daniel Webster Whittle, 1885

Lord, thank You for Your mercy drops as we await
Your flood rains of blessing!

Day 117
Look No Further

But now, Lord, what do I look for? My hope is in You.
Psalm 39:7

What a glorious state of being when we finally realize that everything our heart desires has already been given us in Jesus Christ! There is an eternal rest achieved within our soul when we want for nothing except to personally and intimately know our Savior. Could It be that we can come to a place when even our external circumstances can no longer contend with our affections for the True Love of our lives? This very place of secure love and faith ought to be the crowning achievement against all our vain efforts. What more would we need to look for to satisfy us if we already have placed all our hope in Christ? Would not everything else fall second in line to such a blessed peace and restful revelation? Let us test the loyalty of our hearts and the allegiance of our lives to the One who reigns supreme over all that is seen and unseen. Lord, may we only look for You, lest we waste our energies searching for that which is less worthy. *But now, Lord, what do I look for? My hope is in You.*

Firmly fixed with steady gaze,
Upon Your strength and power.
Accepting all Your glorious grace,
That is with me every hour!
The rest that I've so longed for,
You have mercifully bestowed on me.
And the strain, I now feel no more,

From myself, You've set me free!
What a confidence so blessed,
Yes I can trust You, Lord!
Such a simple faith invested,
Though a value none can afford.
Jesus, Savior, thank You!
Why should You grant this unto me?
A peace, none understanding,
Means more to me than anything!
So guard it with my very life,
What a precious commodity!
Within my soul eternal light,
Whatever Your will, be done to me!

ᴅay 118
Attitude Adjustment

...put off your old self, which is being corrupted by its deceitful desires; to be made new in the attitude of your minds. Do not give the devil a foothold. Ephesians 4:22, 27

There is a reason for putting off our old selves and the deceitful desires of our sinful nature and that reason is to be made new in the attitude of our minds. Becoming more like Christ is the goal to living out the salvation we have received and achieving that goal not only requires a change in our behavior, but a change in our attitude as well. So often we wait for our circumstances to change our mindset, rather than allowing the Spirit of God to change it. If the Spirit is allowed to bring the change or attitude adjustment that we seek, it will come first with an ample dose of conviction. However, it is up to us whether or not we will heed such conviction. If we do not, we will stay with the same negative, downtrodden, even sinful frame of mind and react unwisely to people and things around us. On the other hand, if we do not grieve the Holy Spirit's subtle correction, then even our thought processes will take on that which is of the mind of Christ. Wouldn't we rather think with the attitude of the mind of Christ rather than the mind of the sinful nature? Of course we would, but even this requires a supernatural empowerment which can only come from the Holy Spirit Himself. Therefore, we must humble ourselves before God daily and hide in the shadow of the Almighty. It is only when we try to come out from under that protective shade and shadow of our Savior, that we wind up giving the devil a foothold. A bad attitude exposes us to negative influences and makes us more vulnerable to Satan's attacks. However, Satan cannot gain a foothold if we refuse to stand on his turf! We must stay hidden with Christ in God and allow the Holy Spirit to continually purify our hearts and minds, miraculously imparting to us the mind of Christ.

Attitude adjustment,
Lord, this is what we need!
To heed Wisdom's correction,
As on Your Word we feed!

Attitude adjustment,
Cleanse our sinful minds!
Make us more like Jesus,
Give us the mind of Christ!

Attitude adjustment,
Hide us in Your humble shade.
Of our selfish pride, we lament,
Hidden with Christ, help us to stay!

Day 119
Keep the Peace

...walk in a manner worthy of the calling with which you have been called, with all humility and gentleness, with patience, showing tolerance for one another in love, being diligent to preserve the unity of the Spirit in the bond of peace. Ephesians 4:1-3

Lord, let our walk be faithful,
Filled with humility.
Make little of the trifle,
Not sweating petty things.
Make us worthy of our calling,
Showing gentleness and love.
In all this tolerating,
Aided by the Spirit's dove.
May we ever be so diligent,
To preserve the bond of peace.
Keeping unity in Spirit,
Your sweet fragrance we'll release.
For this life is quickly passing,
The earth's soil soon we'll leave.
Though may we never cease in asking,
Did we love and keep the peace?

Day 120
Humbly Absolved

For thus says the high and lofty One—He Who inhabits eternity, Whose name is Holy: I dwell in the high and holy place, but with him also who is of a thoroughly penitent and humble spirit, to revive the spirit of the humble and to revive the heart of the thoroughly penitent [bruised with sorrow for sin]. Isaiah 57:15, Amp

High and Holy, Lofty One,
Holy is Your name!
Unapproachable, You dwell in light,
Countless hosts declare Your fame!

Glorious, You are, Oh Lord!
None can compare with Thee!
Feared, admired, and adored,
Magnificent indeed!

In all this grandeur we imagine,
How wonderful You are!
Splendor we can't even fathom,
No, our minds can't stretch that far!

Yet amidst the awesome wonder,
What a contrast that we see,
Amalgamation not asunder,
A Holy and humble unity!

Yes, You dwell with the penitent,
To revive the aching soul!
To bring life in such bereavement,

Eternity gripping young and old!

Still bruised with carnal sorrow,
You touch those broken over sin.
Bringing hope to face tomorrow,
Temptations lose, the Spirit wins!

So if this is Your dwelling,
With the broken-hearted man,
Let his pride be oft dispelling,
Bows his knees and lifts his hands!

Then revival with be magnificent,
Between the soul and his great God!
Between the guilty and the innocent,
The highly exalted and humbly absolved!

Day 121
Keep the Standard High!

...however, let us keep living by that same standard to which we have attained. Philippians 3:16

Sadly, in today's generation, we are pulling the high standard, set by the Word of God, down to fit our own individual and lowly average lifestyle. Of course, anyone can keep a standard which never beckons them to rise above the norm! Yet if we continually yearn and strive for a way of life that seeks to glorify God, we will be aided by the Holy Spirit within us to accomplish this goal. It is the indwelling Holy Spirit that will continually connect us to the very presence of Christ. If we only understood how the Spirit of God yearns to lift us up to His higher standard, we would be eager to participate! Keep the standard high! Pray for an overwhelming desire to take on the character of Christ within your entire being. Remember that through Christ's blood and your acceptance of His Lordship over your life, you have already attained the same standard which He has set for Himself!

Keep the standard high!
Don't settle, my dear friend.
You're saved, so you must try,
To let the Spirit win!
Keep the standard high!
Yes, you can raise the bar!
And if you listen closely,
You'll find Jesus is not far!
Keep the standard high!

All the power is within.
The Spirit is your guide,
He'll never lead you into sin.
Keep the standard high!
Don't live what you can see.
Lift your hands up to the sky,
From worldly bondage, be set free!

Day 122
Mercy Cry

Turn to me and have mercy on me, as You always do to those who love Your name. Psalm 119:132

Do you love Him today, my dear friend? If so, then He has no reason not to extend His mercy to you in the very situation that has you confounded and confused. So often we try to figure out why we are facing certain circumstances that have befallen us, or those we love, and we feel compelled to lay the blame somewhere, even if it is on ourselves. But rather than hold onto the struggle in vain, we can cry out to God for mercy. Enduring mercy! We serve a God who does not run out of patience and is longsuffering, willing and waiting to show us mercy. The Psalmist David said, *have mercy on me, as You always do to those who love Your name!* Why not cry out for that which we cannot earn or deserve, even if we try to bring Him our very best? Even our best is as filthy rags in the presence of such Holiness! Cry out in humility and receive that which your soul is longing for in order to set your spirit aright and bring peace to your anxious heart!

Mercy, yes, sweet Jesus,
You are merciful to me.
Your blessed loving—kindness,
It's what untangles me.
Bound by life's hard judgment,
Wrecked by all life's cares,
But then You turn Your ear to me,
And mercy is right there.

Thank You, oh my Jesus,
I don't deserve Your love.
I cannot say I'm worthy,
Your mercies undeserving of.
Yet You always freely give it,
While drawing me so close.
So from all the cries I have sent,
Your mercy, I request the most!

Day 123
Victorious in Valor

...in all these things we are more than conquerors through Him who loved us. Romans 8:37

Do you know you're more than—
So much more than this?
Do you know you're in a legion,
Fighting a battle you can't dismiss?

Do you know you are a conqueror?
Yet even more than that,
You're a child and a Kingdom heir,
By salvation, it's a fact!

Do you know you have a Commander,
Whose gone before you in the fight?
Who is silencing enemy slander,
By His Word and power and might!

Then go forth, my fellow soldier!
Do not sit back in fear!
The struggle will soon be over,
The return of our Savior is near!

There's no need for you to wallow,
Mired in self-defeat.
When the waters are not shallow,
Jesus will meet you in the deep!

So be victorious in valor,
In cadence to Jesus sing!

There is never need to cower,
For we follow a conquering King!

Day 124
He's Calling You

Jesus stopped and said, "Call him." So they called to the blind man, "Cheer up! On your feet! He's calling you." Throwing his cloak aside, he jumped to his feet and came to Jesus. "What do you want Me to do for you?" Jesus asked him. The blind man said, "Rabbi, I want to see." Mark 10:49-51

If we read this whole passage, we would see that blind Bartimaeus began shouting when he heard Jesus was near, saying, "Jesus, Son of David, have mercy on me!" (10:47) This desperate cry caused the Savior to stop and say to His disciples, "Call him." Excitedly, they shouted to Bartimaeus, "Cheer up! On your feet! He's calling you." Oh beloved, today Jesus summons the Holy Spirit saying, "Call him" and "Call her!" When He calls, how do we respond? Do we toss everything aside and jump to our feet in eager expectation of receiving His mercy? Notice that when the blind man came to Jesus, Jesus said to him, "What do you want Me to do for you?" Oh, that we would go to Him, carrying all our burdens to Him and asking Him to open our eyes to the plan He has preordained for us. He is waiting and asking what He can do for us! Lord, let us yearn for Your presence and desire for You to ask us when we cry out to You, "Child, what can I do for you?"

Cheer up! On your feet!
My friend, He's calling you!
Stand up! Leave your seat!
What would you have Him do?
To the Spirit, He says "Call her."

Bring her here to Me.
She is My daughter, I, her Father,
Am here to meet her need!
To the Spirit, He says, "Call him."
Bring him here to Me.
I'll lift him up if he has fallen,
Opening his eyes so he can see!

Day 125
Future Fears

Therefore do not worry about tomorrow, for tomorrow will worry about itself. Each day has enough trouble of its own.
Matthew 6:34

Fear not, My dear, an illusion,
The things that might have been.
Since your dreams can be an intrusion,
For you, on the path I'm trying to send.

Let the future hold its own fears,
You cannot grasp the unknown.
Each step, even taken in tears,
Will never be taken alone.

Walk in truth through each situation,
Live in the present with Me for today.
For I will always give clear direction,
If I want you to move or to stay.

But again, lament not the mirage,
The way life could have been.
Since I alone can see the collage—
Of your life from beginning to end!

Day 126
Summer Breezes

...He stirs up His breezes and the waters flow. Psalm 147:18b

Growing up in the foothills of Montana, I learned a great deal about glaciers. Many of these large ice masses keep their form all year around, never melting to the degree of completely losing their shape. And in the sensational summer months of the Big Sky, one can still gaze upon snow–capped mountains due to their arctic sustainability. However, more than their being white cotton patches high upon the Mission Mountains, these glaciers provide clean, cleansing refreshment. Every stream and lake for miles under the umbrella of the icy accumulation gives its credit to the glacier runoff during the warm summer months. This crisp, clear, brilliantly blue mountain water, found in the most hidden and tranquil oasis spots, provides necessary nourishment to sustain all wilderness wildlife. And if it were not for those warm summer breezes, threatening to utterly liquefy the solid and steadfast mountainous fixture, it would never have the opportunity to offer such satisfying streams. We have been made secure in Christ and others look to the steady strength found in our foundation. The breezes the Lord sends our way from time to time serve to merely allow the waters of the Spirit to flow into the lives of those around us. These seemly threatening gusts cannot be stirred by themselves since they must heed the command of their Master. Therefore, never fear, my dear friend, though the heat and the wind seem to dissolve your strength, they will not utterly misshapen you. Your foundation will remain and others will receive life. Accept the gentle winds that have come to blow upon you. You can rest assure that they are there for a reason and only for a season.

The Master's sweetly calling,
The summer breeze to blow.
And melt the icy glaciers,
Along with all the snow.

At once the water rushes,
Down the steep ravines,
And into all the places,
Nourishing from feet to wings.

Then the glacier gives approval,
After seeing waters flow.
Satisfied with some removal,
When the summer breezes blow.

Day 127

Keep On

So our eyes look to the LORD our God, till He shows us His mercy. Psalm 123:2

Keep looking, don't turn away.
Mercy is coming, it might be today!

Keep steady, with eyes above.
The Spirit it ready, He'll descend as a dove!

Keep silent, with a listening ear.
The Word is speaking, for you to hear!

Keep seeking, each day anew.
God is working, He will come through!

Day 128
Help and Shield

What strength do I have, that I should still hope? What prospects, that I should be patient? We wait in hope for the Lord; He is our help and our shield. Job 6:11, Psalm 33:20

Have all your prospects failed you?
Is all your patience lost?
Has all your strength, come to an end,
Hopes and dreams been tossed?

Is your head so filled with questions?
Is your heart so filled with pain?
Are you tired of endless lessons,
Feeling nothing from them gained?

Do you shake your head in wonder,
And say to Him, "Why me?"
Do you awake amidst your slumber,
Wishing for a bed of ease?

Are you tired of the waiting,
Wishing all your faith be sight?
Anxiously anticipating,
To be brought into the light?

Well, my friend, I cannot help you,
I cannot make it all okay.
To say so would not be true,
But please don't be dismayed.

For our hope is not in this life,
It's not in what we see.

It's not in joy or in strife,
Not in any earthly thing.

Our hope alone is Jesus,
He is the Author of our faith.
And all that He sees in us,
Will be revealed one day.

So leave with Him your sorrow,
Take it to His feet.
The questions of tomorrow,
Will dissolve in grace replete.

And in His loving presence,
He will cast out all your fear.
Then you can wait in reverence.
With your help and shield so near.

Day 129
The Truth I Know

...But hope that is seen is no hope at all... Romans 8:24b

Hope, I cannot see you,
Why do you hide from me?
In the midst of all the darkness,
Not a glimmer do I see.

Have you left the place I'm standing?
Have you drifted out of sight?
If I fall, is there safe landing,
When every day feels like the night?

But what if I could see you?
What would that really mean?
Would I feel a little better,
Would it help me to believe?

And if my eyes, they fail me,
Straining only but to see,
Would hope dissolve, diminish,
Based on my validity?

Though my flesh may try to give in,
And the world may try to prove,
That hope can't hold my burden,
Nor make the mountains move.

Yet if I could see or prove you,
Hope, you'd be no hope at all!
And your work would be contingent,
When in life, things rise or fall.

Oh Hope, You are a constant!
Not a feeling or a phase!
Not dependent on life's nonsense,
Not some holiday parade!

Hope, You are all I cling to,
When I see nothing at all!
You are there and when I need You—
You listen when I call.

And even when I'm weakened,
You have a hold of me.
And it's by faith that I am strengthened,
By the truth I know... not see.

Day 130
Deep Water

When He had finished speaking, He said to Simon, 'Put out into deep water, and let down the nets for a catch.' Simon answered, 'Master, we've worked hard all night and haven't caught anything. But because You say so, I will let down the nets.' Luke 5:4-5

How often we exhaust ourselves by laboring in our own strength! We spend long nights in waters which are too shallow to bring about any fruitful results. And along with our endless labor, we carry a weight of anxiety that in itself is heavy enough to sink our weakened little fishing boat. Yet somehow, through all of our vain toiling, we believe that we are being faithful to do our part to provide nourishment for others. Peter and his few fishing companions must have felt this way to some degree as they worked hard all night, but caught nothing. But something that is very crucial to our understanding of today's verses is a phrase which lies just before these. In Luke 5:3, we read that Jesus stepped into Simon's boat prior to telling him where to cast his net. And what does He tell Simon? "Put out into deep water..." Before we can go out into deep waters, where the oceans are teeming with life and blessing, we must first allow Jesus to step into our boat. Then, when we are working with Him at our side, allowing Him to guide us, lead us and instruct us, we will experience results we never even imagined could be possible! Not only will we find success in our endeavors, but we will find rest, since our sweet Companion is right there with us in the boat. Go with Jesus out into the deep waters and cast your net in the place He tells you. And by doing so, you will reap a bounty of blessing!

When they had done so, they caught such a large number of fish that their nets began to break. Luke 5:6

Child, you must be weary,
Working hard all night?
And I can see so clearly,
How your nets are woven tight.

In these shallow waters,
Catching nothing here to show.
To feed the sons and daughters,
Who need nourishment to grow.

So let Me travel with you,
Come closer, to the shore.
And where the water's deep blue,
The blessings will be more!

Day 131
Hidden Faults

But who can discern their own errors? Forgive my hidden faults. Keep your servant also from willful sins; may they not rule over me. Psalm 19:12-13

Lord, are they really worth it,
The sins we hold onto?
Those we know are unfit,
And really hate to do!

Your thoughts are so much higher,
Yes, lofty are Your ways!
How can we be discerners,
In living out our days?

Sinful we are from birth,
Your Word has proved this true.
Your Sacrifice on this earth,
Only could such fate undo.

And by this we're forgiven,
Cleansed and white as snow.
Yet why do we live in sin,
As if we didn't know?

Lord, purge us, give us clean hearts,
A passion for the pure.
For here in these hidden parts,
Satan's crouching at the door.

The way we speak, the way we act,
Lacking sensitivity.

Mindless thoughts floating in black,
Amidst our insecurities.

Though at once we are forgiven,
When we confess all sins to You.
All that which we have hidden,
You will expose the lies with Truth.

Then again You'll be our Master,
Training gently with Your grace,
Bringing our hearts even faster,
To a repentant, humble state.

Day 132
Pondering Heart

Return to rest, O my soul, for the LORD has dealt bountifully with you. Psalm 116:7, NASB

Sometimes the anxieties of our lives can be calmed with a mere moment of quiet contemplation. How has the Lord dealt with you? Allow your thoughts to drift to a time in which you were brought into a spacious place by the redeeming hand of the Almighty, or a time when your soul was comforted after being crushed with sorrow unspeakable. Drift back to that glorious journey when the Holy Spirit brought the saving knowledge of the Lord Jesus Christ into your life and upon your acceptance you were instantly pulled from the clutches of death! Ponder how you have been purchased by the covenant fulfilling blood of Jesus and by His sacrifice, have been birthed into eternal life through the imperishable seed of truth! Imagine still the glory that awaits us and the One whom we will gaze upon in all of His splendor as we take our prepared place in the Heavenly Temple of our God. Quiet your heart and ponder, then return to rest, dear soul, for the LORD has dealt bountifully with you! Place yourself and all that weighs heavily upon you back into the hands of your Keeper, and trust Him to see you through to the end.

Return to rest, O my soul!
What bounty you've received!
Ponder all that you've been told,
In your sadness, still believe!

Throw your weight upon Him,
Lest you fall beneath the load.
All anxieties you must lend,
For the Master's hands to hold.

Then only for a moment,
Let your mind be calmly stilled.
Thinking now of the Atonement,
And all that He's fulfilled!

Child of Kingdom favor,
Forget not whose you are!
Cease briefly now from labor,
And rest with pondering heart.

Day 133
Teach Me

Teach me Your way, Lord; lead me in a straight path... Psalm 27:11

A teachable spirit is one that will never cease to gain wisdom in every season of life. When we encounter difficulties, our first prayer ought to be, "Lord, teach and impart to me all the wisdom I can possibly acquire from what I am experiencing!" Not only should we seek to grow in wisdom but we must also seek the straight path. God so mercifully will keep us on His path, but often it is our choice whether or not that path will lead us according to His perfect will for our lives. Whenever we choose to go ahead of God, even if only for a short time, we invariably make the path much more complex. We weary ourselves through our own anxieties, frustrations, and fears. Then after much exhaustion, we finally pray, "Lord, teach me Your way!" Oh Lord, help us to come to You first, our Rabboni, so that You may teach us Your ways and lead us in the straight path!

Lord, calm my restless spirit,
Grant me peace within,
So I, Your voice, can hear it,
Bring my worries to their end!
I'm tired from the struggle,
And stretched amid the strain,
Though the stress, it may be subtle,
Nonetheless, it still remains.
So teach me in these seasons,

To see Your point of view.
To understand the reasons,
Why my heart must trust in You!
Let me grasp the hidden message,
Teach me wisdom as I wait.
Through the fog of this life's voyage,
My path I trust You to make straight.

Day 134
My Mouth Guard

Set a guard over my mouth, Lord; keep watch over the door of my lips. Psalm 141:3

A guard, that's it! That's what I need,
To watch over my mouth!
To stand, a watchman, taking heed,
From a whisper to a shout!

A tiny, tin armed soldier,
At attention and at ease,
His gaze shoulder to shoulder,
Yet my mouth he always sees!

And though at times I may insist,
That he take leave from me,
May he relay cease and desist,
To remind me of his need!

And when I utter nonsense,
All the things I should not say,
He'll quickly be at my defense,
And remind me just to pray.

I know I'd grow to love him,
Since he'd always save my skin!
Keep me from speaking on a whim,
So many victories we'd win!

So Lord, since I don't have one,
One of these little, tiny guards.
Can You remind me how Your Son—

Stayed silent at all costs?

Mocked, spit on, and beaten,
He uttered not a sound.
His life constantly threatened,
Yet in Him no sin was found.

So when I start to say things,
I know I should not say,
I will choose to be an offering,
That submits to You this day.

Also choosing to be silent,
Even when it's hard.
With my words never be violent,
Lord, will You be my mouth guard?

Day 135
Christ In Me

But in your hearts set apart Christ as LORD. Always be prepared to give an answer to everyone who asks you to give the reason for the hope that you have. But do this with gentleness and respect. 1 Peter 3:15

Sharing Christ with those around us ought to be as easy as breathing. However, more often than not, it presents for us a challenge. When we look closely at today's verse, Peter gives us the secret to sharing our faith. *But in your hearts set apart Christ as LORD.* If we have truly set apart Christ as Lord in our hearts, then sharing Christ with others should be the same as sharing our hearts with them. Never be ashamed to give full credit to the Lord for all the blessings He has bestowed upon you and your family. Just as equally, never be ashamed to admit your dependency on the Lord in your hardships. When others see that your life is wholly committed to the cause of Christ and He has full Lordship over you, the opportunity to share the very reason for the hope you have, will inevitably present itself. Never mind if you do not receive the response you seek or the approval from those who have yet to put their faith in Christ. Rather, continue to be true to the Lord of your heart and never fail to share Him with others in all gentleness and respect. If your image reflects that of Christ, others will see it and be drawn to Him. Let the Lord of your heart reign in you this day and bring hope to those in darkness!

Lord, fill this mortal body,

With the Spirit from above.
Then let me speak so boldly,
Yet in gentleness and love.

Fill my heart with plenty,
Swell within my veins,
Let my sinful flesh be emptied,
As Christ within me reigns!

Then all around will see it,
Before my lips utter a sound.
And those in need shall benefit,
When Christ, in me, they've found!

Day 136
Greatly Oppressed

...they have greatly oppressed me from my youth, but they have not gained the victory over me. Psalm 129:20

Where lies your oppression? Are you still greatly affected by things or persons who caused you pain in your youth? As you reflect, even in this moment, does that which has had hold of you still remain? From youth, Satan begins to lay a foundation of death in order to trap us in it for life. His purpose is to greatly oppress us while we are young and defenseless. Nevertheless, those of us of in Christ have gained weapons of warfare which we now use to fight and guard against our oppressors. Therefore, we no longer have to fall prey to such attacks! The fight for freedom from sin is a continual battle. Satan wants to make us feel defeated and as if we have been fatally wounded, no longer having access to the healing balm of the Word of God. But we do have access and the power that goes with it! We may not yet be able to entirely stop the enemy from his oppressive operations, thereby gaining victory over him, but we can stop him from gaining victory over us! And we can rest in knowing that our Savior has the ultimate victory over all!

As a child, you oppressed me,
You stole away my youth!
In chains rather than be free,
You feed me lies and not the truth!
Yet with my helmet of salvation,

The Spirit's sword strapped to my side,
I began to use my weapons,
And learned how to win this fight!

Though the battle still is raging,
And still out there, this enemy,
There are lives in need of saving,
He's not gained victory over me!

Day 137
Not A Minute Too Late

...which He will bring about at the proper time—He who is the blessed and only Sovereign... 1 Timothy 6:15

Seasons of waiting can produce a strength in us that can be achieved in no other way, except to simply wait! Waiting tests us to the very core of our character, while reminding us of our own natural limitations. How wonderful to possess the ability to wait with faithful patience upon our Savior! But you see, dear friend, waiting exercises our faith with such precision, that we must be willing to endure it for many seasons throughout our lives. God is never in a hurry. He is never anxious. His ways and His plans are executed with such Divine detail, that doing things any other way would mar His perfect character. God is also Sovereign and has already laid out the course of our lives from beginning to end. He would rather have us be upset for a brief while than to give us our own hasty desires, which if given to us according to our timing, could cause unalterable consequences. He is the blessed and only Sovereign! Shouldn't this truth be enough for us to patiently wait on Him?! Lord, help us to wait upon You, knowing that Your ways are perfect and You have never once lost track of time!

Hold fast, beloved,
He is on His way!
Not a minute too soon,
Not a minute too late!
With Sovereign eyes,

He sees beginning to end.
He won't fail you now,
He's your closest Friend!

So wait in hope,
Let Him strengthen your faith!
One day at a time,
He is working His way!

He knows His plans,
They are written in stone,
And will come to pass,
If you trust Him alone!

Then His light will reveal,
The next step to take,
And you will see it,
Not a minute too late!

Day 138
Full Measure

...to know this love that surpasses knowledge—that you may be filled to the measure of all the fullness of God. Ephesians 3:19

True love is manifested by a truer trust. When we trust God completely, we can love Him despite our lack of knowledge of His workings and His ways. We can trust Him with the things we do not understand or the sufferings we encounter because His infinite love surpasses our finite knowledge. The God of all truth must be trusted by faith, since we have not seen with our own eyes the fulfillment of all that He has promised to bring about in His Word. And yet, if we fully give ourselves over to the abandonment of His Holy Spirit, no longer does our mind long for knowledge, but instead our soul longs to be filled to the measure of all the fullness of God! Thus, when all that we may have mistakenly placed our hope in fails, we are finally ready to take on the very nature of Christ and place all our hope in Him alone. And not only does He Himself become our only hope, but He also becomes our greatest love.

Take me over, me possess!
Head and shoulders,
And all the rest!
Full acquaintance,
With Your power!
Your graciousness,
Felt every hour!
A nearer longing,

To me abide,
Ceaseless love,
From You, I find!
Desperate measure,
Fill fully Thine,
The rarest treasure,
Forever mine!

Day 139
Pushed Back

I was pushed back and about to fall, but the LORD helped me.
Psalm 118:13

Often it can feel as though we are living life against the grain. We take two steps forward and then two steps back. One minute we feel on top of the world, then plunged beneath the depths of the sea the next. Grand fulfillments can so easily yield to grave failures. Sometimes we push ourselves back through our own fleshly tendencies and other times we are pushed back by uncontrolled circumstances or people or all three! Our struggles can thrust us to the very edge uncertainty and threaten to cast us down. Yet, even when hard pressed on every side, we still have a Helper. There is always a divine hand reaching out to pull us back to steady ground. And not only does the hand of the Lord help steady us, but it also strengthens us. Then after being taken hold of, the Lord desires for us to lean forward into Him when we feel as though life is pushing us back. Satan wants nothing more than for us to forget that the Lord is our Helper and our ever present help in time of need (Psalm 46:1). What are you facing today that you could use a divine hand in? Who or what has pushed you back and threatened to make you fall? Do not forget to take the hand that is reaching out to you. It is your only hope!

Frantic arms are flailing!
Lord, I'm about to fall!
I fear that I am failing,

And I have no strength at all!

The edge where I am standing,
All that has brought me here,
It seems there's no safe landing,
I'm giving way to fear!

But with a love unending,
You reach Your hand to me.
Your right arm You are lending,
My eyes begin to see!

With feeble hands I take it,
Though my grasp is very weak,
By my strength I would not make it,
Yet it's Your hand that's holding me.

And as I lean in forward,
Resting all of my frail frame,
I hear You softly whisper,
And kindly say my name.

My child, I have got you,
Lean hard against My frame,
I have the strength to hold you,
Just reach out and call My name!

Day 140
Do Not Hide

You are the light of the world. A city set on a hill cannot be hidden; nor does anyone light a lamp and put it under a basket, but on the lampstand, and it gives light to all who are in the house. Matthew 5:14-15

Lord, we've been appointed,
To be a light for You this day.
By the Spirit, been anointed,
To point others to the Way.

Lord, mercifully You've called us,
To stand out among the crowd.
And it's You alone we've trusted,
To protect us by Your shroud.

Father, when we're tempted,
To run away and hide,
Let us once again be emptied,
Of all our foolish pride.

For soon it will be over,
As eternity awaits.
Keep us alert and sober,
To walk others through Your gates!

And rid us of the baskets,
That dare to hide Your light.
Rather offer us a lampstand,
Anoint more oil to stay bright!

My friend, we are a city,

Set high upon a hill,
Let us not neglect our duty,
But rather, do our Father's will!

Day 141
Protection & Peace

You will guard him and keep him in perfect and constant peace whose mind [both its inclination and its character] is stayed on You, because he commits himself to You, leans on You, and hopes confidently in You. Isaiah 26:3, Amp

Guard us, Mighty Warrior,
Protect us with Your hand,
Keep us in perfect, constant peace,
According to Your plan.

All things to You committed,
Our character inclined,
Self—confidence omitted,
Please grant us peace of mind.

Thoughts rendered ineffective,
Unless they're stayed on You,
Hearts bare and unprotected,
Without the hidden Truth.

Leaning all we have entrusted,
On Your everlasting arms,
The rest of life adjusted,
For a hope with no alarms.

Day 142
Uncompromisingly Righteous

The lips of the [uncompromisingly] righteous feed and guide many... Proverbs 10:21, Amp

What an intriguing concept for those who seek to live with a strict personal integrity! They end up being the ones who guide others in the way of truth by living up to a standard that no one else has set for them except Christ alone. And notice that it's not only a life lived with integrity, but more narrowly, *the lips of the uncompromisingly righteous*. This truth ought to leave us unsettled enough to sift the course of our daily routines, begging God to show us where we have potentially or unknowingly compromised in word or in deed. The underlined motive for us to even engage in such a task, with the aid of the Holy Spirit, is not merely for our benefit, but rather to maximize our usefulness to the lost and hungry souls around us. The effect of our desire for such integrity will never result in a self–righteous ploy, but rather portray the purest form of Christ's love. A love that would rather sacrifice the pleasing of self in order to serve others. Oh Father, open our eyes to where we've compromised and by the power of your Holy Spirit, enable us to selflessly put aside that which may hinder our usefulness in guiding and providing for those in desperate need!

We cannot live without You,
You are greatest help.
You guide us in our servant–hood,
We look to no one else!

But Lord, we're often subject,
To our own sinful way.
And blinded to the effects,
That could lead others astray.

So cleanse us, Holy Father,
Shine Your light of truth,
Reveal where we have wandered,
Compromised or been uncouth.

Then our lips would guide so many,
And feed the hungry souls,
Since as Your vessel we'd be emptied,
Letting Your Spirit take us hold!

Day 143
The Message

See to it that no one takes you captive through hollow and deceptive philosophy, which depends on human tradition and the elemental spiritual forces of this world rather than on Christ. Colossians 2:8

Has someone held you captive,
To a false philosophy,
Making this world more attractive,
Being bound, instead of free?

Have you depended on tradition,
With familiar company,
Accepting spiritual rendition,
In a more comfortable scene?

Has the message become hollow,
Watered down, easily received?
And souls become so shallow,
Living however they well please?

But Christ, He is the Message,
And His Cross is ours to bear,
His life is no mere vestige,
We feel His Presence everywhere!

So if we have His fullness,
There'll be room for nothing else.
We'll consider this world foolish,
Sacrifice it and ourselves.

To live for something greater,

Walk the path of righteousness,
Hand in hand with our dear Savior,
His Lordship our lives will attest!

Day 144
Your Patience

The Lord is not slow in keeping His promise, as some understand slowness. He is patient with you, not wanting anyone to perish, but everyone to come to repentance. Bear in mind that our Lord's patience means salvation... 2 Peter 3:9, 15a

Oh Lord, look at the world today,
It seems the bitter end!
And we can't stand it anymore,
When the enemy seems to win!

There are voices crying out to You,
"Save us from ourselves,
From the present evil reckoning,
And the demons loosed from hell!"

So upside down our worldly view,
The foolishness we see,
Why can't they understand the truth,
And be brought to their knees?!

We cannot go about our days,
As if unable to read or heed,
That Your Word tells us to fast and pray,
Then deliverance we'd see!

Often our cry is, "Come, Lord!
Come quickly, bring us home!"
Yet the tears we'd cry for the unsaved,
There's no returning once we're gone.

We cannot call for Heaven,
While hell's begging for more,
To consume all of the fallen,
Those yet to claim You as their Lord!

If Your patience means salvation,
Then let our hearts say, "Wait!"
And let us boldly claim Your Name,
Changing the beggar's fate!

Lord, thank you for Your patience,
Jesus, that You would wait for me,
For if You had come some years ago,
My sins, to hell, would have followed me!

Day 145

Entering His Rest

There remains, then, a Sabbath-rest for the people of God...
Now we who have believed enter that rest. Hebrews 4:9, 3

Surely, Lord, you have my life,
I submit it unto Thee.
And know that by Your perfect way,
You never cease to meet my need.

So I'll buckle not in darkness,
In Your silence, I'll not fear.
For I know Your plans are flawless,
And Your presence, oh so near.

Shall it always be this easy,
To rest within Your care?
To take a longer, patient road,
One that charges me no fare?

A path that is not strenuous,
To the inner man.
A path never traveled alone,
But forever guided by Your hand.

And this rest that I'm afforded,
By Your precious blood atoned,
Can be received completely,
When I claim Heaven, my home!

Then my soul can seek still waters,
Flowing from Your glorious throne.

As we both sit here together,
No need for other lands to roam.

Day 146
Compromise

But the word is very near you, in your mouth and in your heart, that you may observe it. Deuteronomy 30:14

I had a man named Compromise,
Visit me today.
I must say he was very nice,
Therefore, I let him stay.

As we began our conversation,
Everything seemed fine.
And all that he was saying,
Found confirmation in my mind.

The afternoon kept drifting,
The hours, they passed by,
My spirits they were lifting,
All he said seemed worth a try!

When we gave our salutation,
He kindly went his way.
As I replayed our conversation,
I quickly felt the urge to pray.

Down my cheek I felt tears flowing,
And my heart began to ache.
The knowledge I was holding,
Came from a man who was a fake!

Compromise was not a gentleman,
He was worldly and unwise.
He made things sound so simple and—

To say "no" would be unkind.

Yet stronger words pursued me,
Ones within my heart.
They spoke so very clearly,
When brought out from the dark.

And with my mouth I said them,
These living words of life,
And the message I heard from Him—
Was, "Compromise is never right."

Thank the Lord, the Word is near me!
It's in my heart and in my mind.
And if I listen, very clearly,
I'll hear Truth, not Compromise.

Day 147
Beautify the Soul

For the LORD taketh pleasure in His people: He will beautify the meek with salvation. Psalm 149:4, KJV

What a marvelous thought that the Lord would take pleasure in us! Even when we are so hard on ourselves concerning our lack of faith and numerous shortcomings, our Father still delights in us. He is proud of us! He loves us and is merciful toward us. If we could only grasp the depth of His love! We have a Father whose heart turns within Him over the state of His people. He beautifies, with salvation, those who humbly accept His sacrifice and Lordship by faith. In fact, He is so eager to *beautify the meek,* that He will often allow those whose hearts He is looking to fully capture to be broken in order to be eternally mended. So take heart, my dear friend, your soul is in gentle, healing hands. One day we will see the beautiful work He has been crafting into our hearts and it will be perfect!

Take heart, dearest sister,
The Lord delights in you!
He hears your faintest whisper,
And answers You with truth.

Take heart, faithful brother,
Your Fathers' pleased indeed.
You'll find acceptance with no other,
Only He can meet your need.

The Lord, He takes pleasure,

In those He calls by name.
Each one is His rare treasure,
And forever, they'll remain.

He gives grace to the humble,
And beautifies the meek.
He finds favor with the gentle,
While strengthening the weak.

So take heart, broken child,
Your Father sees your pain.
All your tears He has filed,
To return as healing rain.

Yes, He'll bring eternal mending,
To the desperate, young, and old.
Whether sealed or need of saving,
He seeks to beautify your soul!

Day 148
Nightly Communion

...commune with your own hearts upon your bed and be silent.
Psalm 4:4b, Amp

There is nothing more valuable than to truly meditate upon God's Word and His ways while lying upon our beds at night. In the stillness and silence, at the close of the day, we are given the opportunity to allow the Spirit of God to search our hearts and either commend or convict our actions. If we are humble enough to allow such access of our souls to the blessed Counselor, He will speak to our wandering, weary, anxious hearts and minds. What a relief to know that if we so choose, we can lay down all that hinders us by night, and wake to a renewed mercy and strength by morning. However, unless we silently, with our own thoughts and opinions aside, commune our hearts to the standard of Christ, we will only drift away into slumber carrying our rebellious natures into the next day. Oh, for the grace to allow our hearts to be sifted in order for the Holy Spirit to carry away the chaff, leaving only the wholeness of the hope we possess through the righteousness of Christ Jesus!

Lay me down, commune with me,
In the conversation of my heart.
As I gather all the day's events,
Thinking back to my morning's start.
There isn't much I need to say,
Only lie here and be still.
My prayer is lent a humble way,

Then I offer a submissive will.
Very softly I can hear Him,
As He begins to speak,
To remind me of all I'd forgotten,
And the moments I felt weak.
I wince and begin to suffer,
Thinking of the mistakes I made.
Perhaps the guidance I ner' offered,
To some who had passed my way.
Or the way I spoke unkindly,
To a loved one, foe, or friend.
Or my actions so untimely,
Perhaps correspondence I didn't send?
But a gentle nudge pursues me,
And calms my anxious mind.
Reminding me of my heart's need,
To be cleansed and then unwind.
Then I speak in full surrender,
"Oh Lord, forgive me please,
I need Your grace unhindered,
To bid my bindings free!"
How merciful a Savior!
How marvelous a King!
Who shows us blessed favor,
Cleansing us to wake and sing!
Thus at night my heart's communion,
Reaps joy abundantly,
Since upon my bed, reunion,
With the Spirit, my Savior, and me!

Day 149
Who Could Stand?

If You, O Lord, kept a record of sins, O Lord, who could stand? But with You there is forgiveness; therefore You are feared. I wait for the Lord, my soul waits, and in His Word I put my hope. Psalm 130:3-5

If You kept a record,
O Lord, who could stand?
For none could afford it—
Sin's high demand!

By sin we are guilty,
And make no mistake,
Righteous acts, they are filthy,
Yet with pride we partake.

By nature we're lawless,
And headed for death.
We are so far from flawless,
A mere vapor, a breath.

If You kept a record,
O Lord, who could stand?
For none could afford it,
Sin's high demand!

But with You, there's forgiveness,
Therefore You are feared,
Even those who were lawless,
Through Christ are revered.

So we wait for You, Lord,

In Your Word, put our hope.
It's our shield and our sword,
Solid anchor, safe rope!

You have saved us from death,
You've absolved all our shame.
And in You, we find rest,
By Your righteousness remain.

So we stand for one reason,
By Your blood, sin atoned,
From death, we've been ransomed,
And it's through Christ alone!

Day 150
Faithful Guide

Because of Your great compassion You did not abandon them in the wilderness. By day the pillar of cloud did not fail to guide them on their path, nor the pillar of fire by night to shine on the way they were to take. He guides me along the right paths for His name's sake. Even though I walk through the darkest valley I will fear no evil, for You are with me.
Nehemiah 9:19, Psalm 23:3-4

On the mountains, in the valley,
You are our faithful Guide!
In the sunshine, in the darkness,
Your face, You never hide!
Though clouds may mask the sunshine,
Smoking fire veil the moon,
Yet the path You'll never disguise,
You guide through rough or smooth.
You sustain us on our journey,
Every step You help us take,
And when we feel most weary,
We go on for Your name's sake.
And through the darkest valley,
When we cannot depend on sight,
And though sounds around us gally,
You stay with us through the night.
Your compassions, Lord, they fail not,
You are our faithful Guide!
With each step, Lord, You have brought—
Us closer to Your side!
And when our journeys' ended,

What a homecoming received!
Hosts and angels all attending,
Praising the Guide whom we believed!

Day 151
Walking in the Dark

...His lamp shone upon my head, and by His light I walked through darkness...Job 29:3 ESV

Every one of us experience seasons of walking in darkness. Either our flesh fails us and we stumble into sin or our trials and griefs plunge us into depths of darkness where there seems to be no light at all. Not only is there no light, but there also seems to be no hope. The last thing we may feel like doing is searching for God when we cannot even see the next step on the path before us. Yet, despite the thick mask of despair threatening to smother us, we cannot help but feel that we are not alone. If we will but speak His name and unfold the pages of His written Word, we will hear Him speak and we will feel His presence all around us. The lamp of His Word will shine upon us and by His light we will walk through our darkest times. We are not to wait with bated breath simply for the light at the end of the tunnel, squinting our eyes in search for a bed of ease, but we are to wait upon the Lord and allow His character to be infused into our being even in the midst of our despair. By allowing Him such liberty with our lives, we will soon see that others, in similar places of distress, will see the light of Christ shining upon us and themselves be soothed and strengthened.

The darkness all around me,
The fear, the grief, despair,
Will never overcome me,

Because I know You're there.
And even when I can't see,
I have Your Word within my heart,
As You speak it softly to me,
Your light shining in the dark.
Then taking one step forward,
I need not be afraid,
Even in the blackest night,
Your light will guide my way!

Day 152
To and Fro

For the eyes of the Lord run to and fro throughout the whole earth, to give strong support to those whose heart is blameless toward Him... 2 Chronicles 16:9a

To and fro, to and fro,
Throughout the earth they go.
Your eyes they range to and fro,
And where they land, it shows!

For the ones on whom they've fallen,
You have granted strong support,
You're the tower they can lean on,
In their storms, You are safe port.

So may our hearts always be blameless,
To receive such strength anew!
And when Your eyes run to and fro,
Find ours already fixed on You!

Day 153
Safely Guarded

By the Holy Spirit who dwells within us, guard the good deposit entrusted to you. 2 Timothy 1:14

You have given a deposit,
My salvation's guarantee,
Granted when I have departed,
Stepping onto Heaven's scene.

And this deposit is Your Spirit,
That dwells within my fame,
When He's speaking, my soul hears it,
Day by day, in me, brings change.

This good deposit You've entrusted,
Must be guarded with great care,
Never let Him be insulted,
By my flesh or other snare.

And though I fight to guard Him,
From the sin that's seeking me,
On His side, I always will win,
Since He's already guarding me!

Day 154
He Will Come!

...say to those with fearful hearts, "Be strong, do not fear, Your God will come with vengeance, with divine retribution He will come to save you." Isaiah 35:4

When we are defenseless, God will deliver us! Oh, the fearful hearts of those who stare in the face of evil and are crushed by the weight of despair! Who will save them? Is it not our God who has given all authority to His Son, Jesus Christ? Will He not stand to His feet at the right hand of the Majesty and look down in righteousness and justice on all that He has created? Where we stand perplexed and powerless, Jesus Christ stands poised and powerful! With an ache and burden heavier than our hearts can fathom, our Lord is carrying the weight of all mankind and the seemingly senseless suffering of His saints upon His heart. Yet the pain endured by those who bear the name of Jesus is carefully recorded and kept sacred in Heaven's treasure trove of love. And the crowns dazzling in brilliant light are being brought out and placed before the throne. Be strong, faithful sons and daughters! Your God will come to save you! You may shed your earthen vessel but take heart, Your God will come with vengeance and divine retribution. He will come to save You, for Your soul will not be kept eternally in the grip of death!

Be strong! Be strong!
In the face of suffering!
Your God will come to save you,

And His angels He will bring!

Fear not, dear beloved,
Though your heart and flesh may fail!
Your God will come to save you,
He will deliver you from this hell!

You may cross Heaven's threshold,
Having tasted death's cruel hate,
Yet your spirit no longer flesh holds,
Your heavenly body now awaits!

And when He comes with vengeance,
With Him, you'll join the battle cry,
Descending from the heavens,
When all see Jesus in the sky!

Day 155
Please Wait

*In their hunger You gave them bread from heaven and in their
thirst You brought them water from the rock...Nehemiah 9:15*

When blinded by the darkness,
Your treasures I will seek!
Like the riches of a sunken ship,
With wonder I will greet!

And though my soul is aching,
My heart within me torn,
You will give me all the comforting,
My longings can afford!

You will feed me bread from Heaven,
I'll drink water from the Rock,
And when all trials, they have left me,
Closer beside You, I will walk!

Day 156
His House

But Christ is faithful as a son over God's house. And we are His house, if we hold on to our courage and the hope of which we boast. Hebrews 3:6

The example we are given in the person of Jesus Christ is absolutely flawless! What a faithful Son God the Father has placed over His House! Christ has dominion over all things and nothing is outside the realm of His control. And by example, we embody Bethel, the House of God, which Jesus oversees with careful, loving, watchful eyes, eyes which range to and fro to strengthen those whose hearts are fully devoted to Him. Though we may possess the strength, have we the courage to be His house? Do we boast of His great name and represent a house of refuge to a lost and dying world? Have we allowed His Holy Spirit to so consume every level, every room, every article of our house and have rightfully given Him the dominion which is already His? He is a faithful son over His house and He is a faithful guardian over us. We can relinquish all control to Him and He will maintain our household with steadfast trust. Oh beloved, He can be trusted with all we are willing to entrust to Him. Hand over the deed, my friend, if you have not already and Christ will never allow His house to decrease in value!

Thank you, Jesus, for Your faithfulness,
A faithful Son over God's house!
And let there be no waywardness,

When we, as Your house, do announce!

You have laid a firm foundation,
One that will never be removed.
And You are building every nation,
Soon Your glory to be proved!

So let this house be steady,
In each of us, You call Your home.
Each room we make ready,
To let Your Spirit freely roam.

May we hold onto the courage,
And the hope that we possess.
May we never feel discouraged,
Remembering how we have been blest!

Yes, Jesus, You are faithful,
A faithful Son over Your house!
Therefore, help us to be faithful,
Lending the deed to no one else!

Day 157
With Me Always

...and be sure of this—that I am with you always, even to the end of the world. Matthew 28:20b

I am sure that You are with me,
You are always by my side.
Even when my heart is aching,
Your sweet Presence, You don't hide.
Sometimes I cannot see You,
Sometimes I feel alone,
But Your Word ever reminds me,
It's in me, You've made Your home.
What would I do without You,
I depend upon You so!
I am weak and I am burdened,
I have nowhere else to go!
But I run right to my Savior,
Through all hours of the night,
He never sleeps, He never tires,
He intercedes to make things right.
Each day I'm walking closer,
Soon I'll gaze upon His face.
Though for now, my heart is consoled,
Knowing He's with me in this place.

Day 158
Overtaken

They will enter Zion singing; everlasting joy will crown their heads. Gladness and joy will overtake them, and sorrow and sighing will flee away. Isaiah 35:10

Lord, let joy overtake us,
As we walk this path of life.
As we journey often desert roads,
And are overcome with strife.

Oh Father, You have promised,
That Your joy we will receive.
As we walk the way of holiness,
With all those who believe.

Though before this journey's over,
Before we reach life's end,
You promised to send flowing streams,
Where we'll never thirst again!

And on the day we enter Zion,
We'll sing songs of the redeemed.
With everlasting joy as our crown,
And from our sorrows, we'll be freed!

Day 159

Heaven's Tabernacle

But when Christ came as high priest of the good things that are now already here, He went through the greater and more perfect tabernacle that is not made with human hands, that is to say, is not a part of this creation. Hebrews 9:11

There is a greater, more perfect tabernacle that exists in Heaven! This tabernacle is not made with human hands, nor is it even part of this creation. No, it is an everlasting place of worship that is reserved for those who have been redeemed by the spotless Lamb of God, whose blood purified more than just tabernacle articles, but rather the whole of the human race. He entered the heavenly Most Holy Place, in the presence of God the Father once for all by His own blood, having obtained eternal redemption for all those who believe (Hebrews 9:12). Praise God that this life is only a dim reflection of the eternal one we were created to live! Our places of worship, from the time of the wilderness tabernacle until now, pale in comparison to the Heavenly tabernacle of the Living God! Imagine those who have gone before us, along with the elders around the throne, bowing in worship and adoration in a house of worship where God Himself is the glorious fixation! And one day soon, that very tabernacle within the Holy City of the new Jerusalem will come "down out of Heaven from God, prepared as a bride beautifully dressed for her Husband" (Revelation 21:2). Then forever we will be His people, God Himself will be our God, and He will wipe away every tear from our eyes. There will be no more death or mourning or crying or pain, for the old order of things will have passed away and the new creation, not made by human hands, will forever remain (21:3-4)!

Oh Glory, Hallelujah!
Righteous, is His name!
Glory, Hallelujah!
The Lamb of God was slain!

He graced us with His presence,
Heaven's High Priest stepped aside.
Coming down to mend our severance,
And again with Him abide!

Now reigning in His temple,
Heaven's perfect worship place,
His atoning work accomplished,
For the entire human race.

And one day we will see it,
The New Jerusalem will come!
Dressed adorned for her Great Husband,
Heaven's worship place, our home!

Day 160
No Shrinking Back

For in just a very little while, "He who is coming will come and will not delay. But My righteousness one will live by faith. And if he shrinks back, I will not be pleased with him." But we are not of those who shrink back and are destroyed, but of those who believe and are saved. Hebrews 10:37-39

Do not shrink back, beloved,
My faithful friend in faith!
For in just a very little while,
Christ will come, He'll not delay!

Don't let Him catch us sleeping,
Or falling into sin.
Don't let Him catch us dreaming,
Our faith unable to defend!

No, God will not be pleased with us,
If we refuse to claim His name.
Living with such self—absorption,
That all we can do is complain.

We will not be those who shrink back!
Those who do not know their call!
Helpless under every attack,
Afraid to rise after they fall!

We will stand firm with our Savior,
We will claim His every Word!
Assured of His eternal favor,
He's our Defender, Sovereign Lord!

Day 161
Altered State

And as He was praying, the appearance of His countenance became altered (different), and His raiment became dazzling while [flashing with the brilliance of lightening]. Luke 9:29, Amp

Jesus prayed with the utmost reverence and undefiled faith! And as He did so, "His countenance became altered." He may have transfigured from a tired, weary, exhausted soul, to one suddenly infused with the power of His Heavenly Father! Jesus was carrying a weight that we simply cannot fathom! His time here on the earth was one of suffering and not only physical, but deeply spiritual. We are told throughout Scripture how Jesus grieved and grieves still for the lost souls who reject His offer of salvation. Yet as He knelt there on the sacred Mount of Transfiguration, He called down His ultimate source of strength given to Him from His Father. The strength and power that exudes from the throne room of grace, was the very substance His soul longed for as He, Jesus, prayed. We too find ourselves in such need of this great reviving sustenance of the soul! As we breathe out utterances to our Savior, we are lifted out of the earthly realm that binds us and transported by the Holy Spirit of God into Heaven's sanctuary of grace. And it is in this place of glory that we are changed more and more into the likeness of Jesus, being given a countenance that radiates His presence amidst a dark and sinful world!
As I kneel upon this rocky knoll,

I gently bow my head,
Resting now my weary soul,
My spirit needing to be fed.

In the stillness of the moment,
What a flood comes over me!
While I wait upon My Savior,
His presence overshadowing!

Then the comfort of all Heaven,
Cradles me and hears my cry,
I have nothing more to question,
I'm no longer asking "why?"

For His Holy confirmation,
Is well enough for me,
Ascending to His elevation,
A calming Spirit settles deep.

And thus arising from this union,
I feel my countenance has changed,
No more lingering confusion,
Only unrelenting grace!

Day 162
None Can Mar

The Lord is in His holy Temple; let all the earth be silent before Him. Habakkuk 2:20

An anxious heart may find great consolation in this verse today! What an astonishing truth that the Lord is in His holy Temple, alive and reigning in power! Nothing is out of order in the entire cosmos. Everything in Heaven and on the earth submits to His sovereign rule. The earth needs only to be still before its Maker. How much more those whom He has chosen to inhabit the whole earth! Let us be silent and stand in awe of His Holiness this day. May our hearts seek the stillness and calming effect of the Lord's prevailing peace. We can trust that He remains in full control over all things. Demand your anxiety, "Be still!" As you stand utterly amazed in the presence of our King!

Lord, You're in Your Holy Temple,
You're reigning now on high!
From the complex to the simple,
You show mercy, You give life!

We have no need to be anxious,
We need only to be still,
Be Christ centered and be selfless,
Resting calmly in Your will.

May we stand here in Your presence,
What an awesome God You are!

We sing praise for all Your goodness,
Your sheer beauty, none can mar!

Day 163
Wholesome & Loathsome

Do not let any unwholesome talk come out of your mouths,
but only what is helpful for building others up according to
their needs, that it may benefit those who listen. Ephesians
4:29

I have an interesting decision,
One to make for each new day.
Which two companions I will carry—
With me along the way.

These attendants have a name,
To describe their expertise,
One is Wholesome, one is Loathsome,
And I choose from both of these.

If I choose them both together,
Loathsome tends to take the lead,
And Wholesome gets left stranded,
Lagging behind Loathsome and me.

Yet He doesn't get discouraged,
Or beg to come with me,
He just sits and waits so patiently,
Underneath a shady tree.

Whereas Loathsome, he's more hasty,
Making sure I know he's there.
But it's not like he's supportive,
I don't think he really cares.

Because every time I'm with him,

He tends to weigh me down,
And even those around me,
Seem to turn away and frown.

He has an awful disposition,
He is selfish and unkind.
And with a nasty inclination,
He pollutes my heart and mind!

Why do I even choose him,
At the start of each new day?
I should leave him in the gutter,
And it's in there, he should stay!

Wholesome, He's the one I'm needing,
He's the one who really cares,
He is never, ever heavy,
Never a burden, nor a snare.

He is very kind to others,
He builds them up and meets their needs,
He is very quick to listen,
Noticing everyone He sees.

He even points me to My Savior,
He always gives me love for Him,
With Wholesome I live in obedience,
When choosing him, I win!

So tomorrow is a new day,
I think I'll leave Loathsome behind,
Keeping Wholesome close beside me,
For with Him, my countenance shines!

Day 164

Recognize

He was in the world, and though the world was made through Him, the world did not recognize Him. John 1:10

How often we can't see, past the nose upon our face!
Much less even recognize, the Creator of the human race!
His presence all around us, His Spirit lives and breathes,
But in all preoccupation, we forget all that He sees.
And we go about our business, in the hustle of this life,
Instead of slowing down to listen to the still, small Voice inside.
If He were walking here among us, would we recognize Him then?
We'd say, "If we could only see Him, then our hearts, He just might win!"
Although how blessed we are believing, in that which we can't see,
Knowing by faith, He's still revealing, in us His true identity!
And we live among a people, who can't recognize their King,
Underneath a cloud of darkness, Satan's overshadowing.
Yet our hearts shall not grow weary, no, we shall not grow faint,
For we are living not for this world, since eternity awaits!
So as we look beyond the lens, of this unbelieving realm,

And in submission we allow, Him our lives to
overwhelm;
We will understand His workings and begin to
recognize,
Everything that He is doing, in His Sovereign, perfect
time.
When He gathers all His children, when He calls them
all by name,
And we leave this world of chaos, to see peace
forever reign!

Day 165
Revival

Will You not revive us again, that Your people may rejoice in You? Psalm 85:6

Revival comes when we lay down our rights,
When with confessing lips, we sum up the nights.
When we choose to belong to alone, Jesus Christ,
And abandon our nature, to the Spirit's great plight!

When we no longer consider ourselves as our own,
And much of our time is spent near His throne.
When temptations of earth defile our mind,
We simply refuse to let such waste our time.

When we refuse self—absorption, refuse our own
name,
Refuse the allure of self—honored fame.
When we humble our hearts for such greater gain,
To see Christ glorified, even in the mundane.

So rise up, dear children, let revival come alive,
Let the blessed Holy Spirit consume your whole life!

Day 166
Yoke Shopping

It is for freedom that Christ has set us free. Stand firm, then, and do not let yourselves be burdened again by a yoke of slavery. Galatians 5:1

Do not let yourselves be burdened! How interesting that we have a choice in the matter! So many people stay bound by a yoke of slavery that has already been removed through Christ's atoning sacrifice. Oh, but how Satan loves to take us shopping for heavy yokes, especially if he sees we don't have one around our neck! In fact, he seems to have every type imaginable for us to choose from. There is the yoke of addiction, fear, anxiety, anger, discouragement, insecurity, dissatisfaction, and the list goes on and on! Not only are there so many different ones to choose from, but there are different sizes too! Satan is a master measurer and takes great time and patience in making sure whichever yoke you choose to wear, it fits you just right. Now we can continue to go shopping with Satan and allow our sinful nature to rack up a credit full of heavy yokes, or we can choose one and keep it on for life. Jesus says in Matthew 11:29-30, *Take My yoke upon you and learn from Me, for I am gentle and humble in heart, and you will find rest for your souls. For My yoke is easy and My burden is light.* The Holy Spirit will adjust us very quickly to the light and easy yoke of Christ. Therefore, when we are tempted to take another yoke upon us, we will urgently seek to remove it. Through genuine repentance, prayer, believing God's Word, and having a desire to be gentle and humble in heart, we will be victorious in untying heavy yokes of bondage. Today, my friend, may just be your day to lighten up!

Let's go shopping, my sweet lady,
I have some yokes right here, they're new!
I'm sure you'd like to try them on,
I've fit them just for you!
Oh here's one, darling,
Try this on!
The label says, Despair.
I knew that you would like it,
Yes, this one you should wear!
Oh here's another,
Discouragement!
How good this looks on you!
It even seems to match your eyes,
A beautiful pale blue!
Ah, but I have saved this last one,
Especially for you!
In case you wanted to be bold
Or try anything new,
Like standing up for Jesus,
Or fully believing in His truth.
We fitted it this season,
To match your latest style,
And if you'd like to wear it,
It will last you quite a while.
We haven't changed the name,
There's really no need to,
Sometimes it's hard to recognize,
But it will look so good on you!
It's fear! Yes, you guessed it,
That's exactly right!

For if I can make you afraid, my dear,
You could wear this day and night!
This yoke, it's very heavy,
Because there are so many parts,
And they can strongly fasten,
To your head and to your heart!
It can even paralyze you,
Some days, you might not move!
But that's okay, my sister,
You need to rest, don't you?
I'll take cash or credit,
Whichever you would like,
Or I can make you indebted,
By restricting your whole life.
Yet if you do not take it,
There's nothing I can do,
I'll just come around next season,
Unless another yoke you choose.

...Stand firm, then, and do not let yourselves be
burdened again by a yoke of slavery." Galatians
5:1b

Day 167

A Panoramic View

"I am the Alpha and the Omega," says the Lord God, "who is, and who was, and who is to come, the Almighty." Revelation 1:8

God is ruler over all! He is ruler over every circumstance. He is ruler over every dark force that seeks to pervade our lives. His desire was initially for us to never possess the knowledge of evil nor suffer its damaging effects. Yet knowing that our hearts would be inclined to choose sin, He still, in His love, looked to the future, and provided a way for us to return to His Lordship. Out of a rebellious heart we flee from adhering to strict obedience in following God's commands. We choose to trust our own judgment and rely on our own knowledge as we live out each day. We scarcely recall the past and we are blinded from the future. Yet we seek to marry our past, present, and future though dependence upon our futile, earthly wisdom. Still there is among us the presence of the Almighty! The Alpha and Omega speaks for Himself here in Revelation as the One who is, who was, and who is to come! Such knowledge, such profound wisdom can only be found in a God who sees from beginning to end. Therefore, my sweet companion in the faith, look to the One whose view is panoramic to your circumstances today. When you can only see but a flicker of hope in the midst of darkness, trust the One whose very essence is brighter than the fullness of the sun!

He sees it all from beginning to end,
And will see us through time and again.
His mercy is great, His wisdom is grand,
He will never leave, or let go of your hand.

The Alpha, Omega, the First and the Last,
He triumphed in victory, glory surpassed.
He chose to forgive us, He provided a way,
We can trust Him tomorrow, and even today.

In His knowledge and wisdom, He brought forth the light,
And soon we'll experience a day with no night!
So until that day comes, we can trust His great plan,
Even trust Him with the things we don't understand.

Day 168
Choosing Him

But God chose what is foolish in the world to shame the wise;
God chose what is weak in the world to shame the strong...
1 Corinthians 1:27

Does this verse find you in the state it describes? Are you confounded as to why the Lord has allowed you to walk through the season you currently find yourself in? At times we tend to think that our preparation for a season of difficulty ought to come equipped with a certain measure of strength for the task. Yet when we find ourselves worn out and weary, discouragement sets in and we are overwhelmed by the insecurity of our lack of ability to continue on. We immediately wish the whole situation would somehow disappear into thin air and that we could forget the whole matter. Or better yet, we spend much time hoping for a scenario that better fits what we feel our level of strength would suffice. You may be asking the question, "Lord, why did You chose me for this?" What a sweet dichotomy we read in our verse for today! God chose you for the season you are experiencing because you are foolish and weak and unable to handle the very thing you are trying so desperately to handle! If He never pressed us beyond our own natural ability, we would never understand His infinite grace, His undeniable power, and His overwhelming mercy so beautifully displayed on our behalf. You were never meant to possess the power to overcome your state of contention by sheer human nature. In fact, the more you rely on a self–imposed strength, the greater the room for error! Therefore, rely on the Lord and His mighty strength! *For the foolishness of God is wiser than men, and the weakness of God is stronger than men (1 Cor 1:25).* He chose you, so that through the humility of your own limitations, You would chose Him!

What strength! What valor!
What Majesty unfolds!
What tranquility, what peace,
What a delicate repose!

Laying down in surrender,
I open my eyes,
And there, up above me,
The vast, open skies!

With my heart overflowing,
I find joy once again,
Calm, collected, and knowing,
He chose me, I choose Him!

Day 169
Lean Not

Trust in the Lord with all your heart, and do not lean on your own understanding. Proverbs 3:5, ESV

I depend not on myself,
Not on giftings of my own,
Not on poverty or wealth,
Not on this temporary home.

I depend not on the seasons,
For they quickly come and go.
I depend not on mere reason,
Or the fight for self–control.

I lean not on understanding,
On my finite capacity,
On the world's constant demanding,
To live by its godless creed.

And I will not give into darkness,
When the way I cannot see,
But I will walk in truth, regardless,
Trusting my God will carry me.

Day 170
I Need You More

But as for me, I am poor and needy...Psalm 70:5

When the heat beats down,
And my soul is dry,
My eyes, they drown,
In the tears I cry,
And I limp along,
As the days gone by,
I need You more, my Jesus.

When the cool winds blow,
And a chill takes me,
But I find relief,
In the colors I see,
And I shelter beneath,
Your loving wings,
I need You more, my Jesus.

When the blankets white,
Frost the window panes,
And I stay inside,
Avoid icy rains,
Yet melancholy,
My heart remains,
I need You more, my Jesus.

When the beauty of—
The springtime comes,
And the birds sing out,
A heavenly song,
And my heart it leaps,

With angelic throngs,
I still need You more, my Jesus!

Day 171

Quiet Retreat

You're my place of quiet retreat; I wait for your Word to renew me. Psalm 119:114, Message

There's a peace that's come upon me,
It lingers in my soul,
And when I cannot understand,
It's Your peace that makes me whole.
It's the love that's all around me,
It's the longing in my heart,
It's the time spent with my Savior,
It's His message in the dark.
It's the silence of the morning,
It's the burden of the day,
It's the way my spirit lingers,
It's the Voice saying, "It's okay."
It's thinking I won't make it,
And just simply can't go on,
Yet it's the Presence here beside me,
That keeps me going strong!

Day 172
When Jesus Comes!

I will... make the valley of Achor into a door of hope. Hosea 2:15

My mother used to sing an old hymn called, *There'll Be No Dark Valley*. As a child, I could not grasp the depth and richness of such a hymn, much less the eternal hope the melody possessed. Yet what brought even more sacred significance to the song, was that she would sing it while leading a small congregation on a Native American Indian reservation in worship. In her beautiful, Tennessee-bred accent, my mother mastered the Navajo translation of this hymn and sang it out with a robust joy and faith that could not be contained. And while many of those in attendance softly sang with solemn face, in their hearts they began to believe that the message of Jesus, relayed from this sweet Southern woman, was true. Many of us walk through dark valleys of sorrow and sadness, but through His sacrifice, Jesus has made Himself our door of hope. *I am the door; if anyone enters through Me, he will be saved, and will go in and out and find pasture* (John 10:9). One day, our feet, which have trod in the dark valleys of this life, will enter into glory though Jesus, our door of hope! And the message of this very hymn, fulfilled now in the life of my sweet mother, will one day be fulfilled in ours as we too will see that *there'll be no dark valley when Jesus comes!*

There'll be no dark valley when Jesus comes,

There'll be no dark valley when Jesus comes;
There'll be no dark valley when Jesus comes,
To gather His loved ones home.
To gather His loved ones home (safe home),
To gather His loved ones home (safe home);
There'll be no dark valley when Jesus comes,
To gather His loved ones home.
There'll be no more sorrow when Jesus comes,
There'll be no more sorrow when Jesus comes;
But a glorious morrow when Jesus comes,
To gather His loved ones home.
There'll be no more weeping when Jesus comes,
There'll be no more weeping when Jesus comes;
But a blessed reaping when Jesus comes,
To gather His loved ones home.
There'll be songs of greeting when Jesus comes,
There'll be songs of greeting when Jesus comes;
And a joyful meeting when Jesus comes,
To gather His loved ones home.

There'll Be No Dark Valley, Hymn,
William Cushing, 1823

Day 173
My Cross

Then Jesus said to His disciples, "Whoever wants to be my disciple must deny themselves and take up their cross and follow Me." Matthew 16:24

My cross I received to carry,
When He said, "Come follow Me."
When my old self, died and buried,
And from my sin, He set me free!

Now at first it was not heavy,
My cross...what a sweet release!
The burden, I felt it barely,
The weight of sin had been heavier to me!

Though the longer, my cross, I carried,
The heavier it became.
And so often I struggled and tarried,
The load of my cross began to change.

But just when I wanted to give up,
And lay my cross aside.
He said, "Daughter, come and with Me sup,
Let's ponder what I've assigned.

I know the cross feels heavy,
You see, I've fashioned it this way.
Though with a gentle hand, I steady,
If the added weight causes it to sway.

The burdens I've placed upon you,
Are to Me no burdens at all.

They are that which I use to fine tune,
Ridding your sinful nature flaws.

The cross gets heavier through trials,
Though never more than you can hold.
Each passing through refining fires,
Producing virtues more precious than gold.

So what I am placing upon you,
Are ornaments from Heaven's tree.
Which I adorn for only a chosen few,
Though there's plenty to give, you see."

Then I said, "Oh Lord, please forgive me!
How foolish I have been!
I've refused ornaments from Your holy tree,
Will You forgive me of this sin?!

If only I had realized,
That with these trials, You decorate me!
Then I never would have despised,
That which reveals Your true beauty.

Oh now, My Lord, I see it!
How lovely is my cross!
By trials, You have made it fit,
Securing its glory, no ornament lost!"

Day 174

Submission Assigned

Nevertheless, each one should retain the place in life that the
Lord assigned to him and to which God has called him...
1 Corinthians 7:17

Is it true You have assigned me,
This humble, quiet place;
A heart You have aligned to Thee,
And as flint, have set my face?

Away from all the hurried crowds,
Just sitting in the leaves;
An unhindered view of all the clouds,
Though not yet gathering the sheaves?

Alone and in such solitude,
With the sudden urge to run;
Yet submitting every attitude,
To see finished, Your work done.

Sitting here, though not alone,
This is something You have wrought.
To my heart Your presence shown,
For it is Your face I have sought.

Trusting now and waiting,
These virtues nourish me.
Your voice anticipating,
A glimpse of glory I might see!

No kinder would a Master—
Dare to place me here.

No gentler would a Pastor,
Let my heart give way to fear.

Now assigned I am this humble place,
Here I am among the leaves.
Yes, it is a quiet space,
Though not yet gathering the sheaves.

Lovely, however, just the same,
For in full view the Master sees;
And with His voice, He calls my name,
By my answer He is pleased.

Now what once seemed lowly solitude,
Becomes quite an honored place!
For you see, a submissive attitude,
Brings a smile to His face!

Day 175
The Fold

Why do You hold back Your hand, Your right hand? Take it from the fold of Your garment and destroy them. Psalm 74:11

Lord, give us the faith to believe in Your awesome power! As You rest in the calmness of Your presence, hands folded, gazing at all that unfolds in the breath of space and time, see Your people and hear their cry! Meet the desperate need for salvation, ready to be received in the sight of all mankind. Creation longs for Your return. Remove Your mighty hand from the fold of Your garment and save! We repent of our wrongdoing and bow before You, Lord. You are mighty to save! Oh, that we would look beyond ourselves to the power that radiates from Your throne! Do we ever have a need that cannot be met or an enemy that cannot be defeated by Your righteous right hand?! Give us faith to believe in our God who is patiently waiting to act on behalf of His children!

A throne of power is Your rest,
You sit, though never tire.
Hand of power beneath Your chest,
Patiently await the hour!
A godless people who never believe,
And anxiously shake their fists.
Wondering at the mess we've made,
Though never do we repent.
Muster your strength, O people of God!
Look to the Man on high!
See Him stretch forth His mighty hand,

Before Him, cherubim fly!
To crush the foe, to break the chains,
To set the captives free!
And by His strength, bring forth His name,
His Kingdom soon we'll see!

Day 176
In All Things

And we know that in all things God works for the good of those who love Him, who have been called according to His purpose. Romans 8:28

One of the greatest challenges in the Christian faith is continuing to love and trust the Lord despite what seems to be unanswered prayers. We may pray desperately for something, whether big or small, but never receive an answer even close to what we have asked for or in the timing we feel we need. So what do we do then? How are we supposed to feel toward God? Thankfully, God, in His unyielding compassion and love for us, understands the trials and challenges we face in this life. He sympathizes with us in ways we simply cannot comprehend. He gave us strong emotions and knows that those emotions can be extremely difficult to harness while living in our sinful nature. So when we are angry or upset at Him for what we feel is unanswered prayer, He sympathizes with that too. The goal for us, when faced with such perplexing uncertainty, is to be reminded that our love for Christ must supersede our immediate circumstances. In our hearts, we must, by the aid of the Holy Spirit, default all negative emotion into submission. We must simply say, "Lord, I do not understand why You will not answer, but despite what I don't understand, I trust You love me and have my absolute best in mind." Then we must look around and back over the course of our lives at all that He has blessed us with. All He *has* answered and all the things we *have* been given that we never even thought to pray for! And then we cling to this truth for today, as we have so many times before: *And we know that in all things God works for the good of those who love Him, who have been called according to His purpose (Romans 8:28).* And in all things, He will hold us together.

When upon life's billows you are tempest tossed,
When you are discouraged, thinking all is lost,
Count your many blessings, name them one by one,
And it will surprise you what the Lord hath done.

Are you ever burdened with a load of care?
Does the cross seem heavy you are called to bear?
Count your many blessings, every doubt will fly,
And you will keep singing as the days go by.

So, amid the conflict whether great or small,
Do not be disheartened, God is over all;
Count your many blessings, angels will attend,
Help and comfort give you to your journey's end.

Count your blessings, name them one by one,
Count your blessings, see what God hath done!
Count your blessings, name them one by one,
And it will surprise you what the Lord hath done.

Count Your Blessings, Hymn,
Johnson Oatman Jr., 1897

Day 177

Song in Sorrow

And the ransomed of the Lord shall return, and come to Zion with songs and everlasting joy upon their heads: they shall obtain joy and gladness, and sorrow and sighing shall flee away. Isaiah 35:10

Sing out a song in sorrow,
Sing out a song of praise!
For you know not of tomorrow,
Nor the full length of your days.

Sing out a song eternal,
Sing with all your might!
And all your pain surrender,
As you grip Jesus' garment tight!

Sing with all the angels,
For one day you will see,
This earth will be a stranger,
And in familiar arms you'll be!

Day 178
Gathering the Lilies

My lover has gone down to His garden to the bed of spices, to browse in the gardens and to gather lilies. Song of Songs 6:2

What a stunning flower, the lily. Its fragrance so bold and so soothing to the senses. Just as our Lord browsed among His garden in the time of Adam and Eve, so His presence does today. He comes "down to His garden"— a garden He has planted first by using rich soil, then cultivating and turning it, in preparation for the seed. A garden He has tended, walking among it before anything began to grow, having kept a watchful eye on its beginnings. A garden He has weeded, pruned, prepared for spring when the blossoms of the flowers were in full bloom and the spices yielded their most fragrant aromas. A garden that has brought Him pleasure during times of resting from His work. And when it is time to gather the lilies, He takes great care in choosing which ones to bring home. These are not just any lilies, these are the lilies whose time of beauty in the garden has reached such perfection that they now must be displayed in the only place where their true radiance and aroma will be eternally admired. They will no longer have to weather the storms of the seasons, nor will they have to lie dormant in the wintertime. The earth's soil will no longer be the nourishment for the roots, for now the time has come for them to take their place on the mantle of Heaven, forever radiant before the eyes of their King.

Father, I know that You must tend—
To the garden of my life.
A work that's done with perfect love,
Though at times I feel the knife!

But please do not stop working,
For I know You're making me,
A lily of perfection,
For all eternity to see!

Day 179
Deep Calls

*Deep calls out to deep in the roar of Your waterfalls; all Your
waves and breakers have swept over me. Psalm 42:7*

Deep calls out to deep,
The rushing of Your waves—
Crash me upon the breakers,
But still my spirit craves...

Craves Your Mighty Presence,
Craves Your still, small Voice,
Begs for Your possession,
This longing leaving me no choice...

But to plunge into Your waters,
Lord, free me from myself!
Take me where your Spirit hovers,
Wanting You and nothing else!

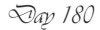# Day 180
How Can I Repay?

How can I repay the LORD for all His goodness to me? I will lift up the cup of salvation and call on the name of the LORD. I will fulfill my vows to the LORD in the presence of all His people. Psalm 116:12-14

Hands lifted high, on my knees, now my face,
How heavy is Your presence, here in this place!
Oh Lord, please use me, that's my only plea,
How can I repay You, after all You've done for me?
I'll do anything You ask, You've forgiven me so much,
How can I say 'I love You,' from this heart You have touched?
But more than just touch, Lord, You are overwhelming me,
How can there be anything, which I prefer over Thee?
This cup, emptied and broken, to You alone I lift,
How can You accept such a weak and meager gift?
But it's all that I can offer, I have nothing else to give,
How can I repay You, for this life I now live?
What's this? A new cup, now poured out unto me?
How glorious to replace my weak and broken entity!
The cup of salvation! Underserved, it sets me free!
Given back to You, my Savior, for the whole world to see!
In the presence of all people, let Your glory now be shown!
Jesus Christ, Blessed Redeemer, Your name I vow to make it known!

Special Devotions
For Christmas & New Years

Christmas

Handmaiden of the King

And he came to her and said, Hail O favored one (endued with grace,) the Lord is with you! Blessed —favored of God —are you before all other women. Then Mary said, "Behold, I am the handmaiden of the Lord..." Luke 1:28, 38 Amp

What an honored greeting for such a young woman and given by an angel of God nonetheless! What had she done to earn such a title? She must have been very righteous and close to sinless to have been handpicked for such a task! We might be tempted to think as such, but Mary was chosen because of her genuine humility to the Lord. Even after such an esteemed welcome, she still saw herself as merely a *handmaiden* or a female slave, ready to do anything her Master asked of her. At the risk of being misunderstood, even by her betrothed husband, she still served her Master. She was willing and ready to allow her body, mind and soul to be led by the Holy Spirit without hesitation. *"How will this be," Mary asked the angel, "since I am a virgin?"* (Luke 1:34). Even in asking Gabriel this question, her greatest fear may have been her inability to fulfill this awesome task. Oh sweet friend, are you like Mary and afraid that you will not be able to accomplish the things God has ordained for your life? Mary had no idea how highly favored she was. In her mind, she was merely a handmaiden of the Most High. Little did she realize that this was the very attitude for which she was held in such high esteem. God merely needed a vessel, a tender child to bear His Son. We do not have to have to wait for an esteemed welcome before we bow down to our Master and offer ourselves to Him as His handmaid, ready and willing to do anything He asks of us.

Blessed is she who has believed that what the Lord has said to her will be accomplished! Luke 1:45

Christmas

Bethlehem's Story

But you, Bethlehem Ephrathah, though you are small among the clans of Judah, out of you will come for Me, One who will be ruler over Israel, whose origins are from of old from ancient times. Micah 5:2

Bethlehem Ephrathah, what a story you have to tell,
From days of old and ancient times,
A story you know well.
Patriarchic beginnings, his beloved resting there,
When Jacob brought his Rachel,
Placing her body in your care.
Bethlehem Ephrathah, 'House of Bread,' that is your name,
Naomi, Boaz, and faithful Ruth,
Also shared your fame.
Six miles from Jerusalem, the prophet Samuel trod,
To seek out sons of Jesse,
And to David, give the nod.
A gentle, humble shepherd, looking after sheep,
Played the harp so sweetly,
Lulling King Saul to sleep.
Bethlehem Ephrathah, town of David, that you are!
Just a boy, some stones, a sling,
And his fame spread near and far.
Elhanan and Asahel, mighty soldiers too,
Were raised up on your sacred lands,
Great honor they accrued.
The Philistines, their garrison, camped on your domain,
But guard your well, they could not do,
And by that, a cup was gained.

Though David did not drink it, He longed to sip it still,
Yet considered himself unworthy,
And to His Father, let it spill.
Bethlehem Ephrathah, in your enemies rushed,
Babylon bondage stole your pride,
Children silenced, captives hushed.
Abandoned was your humble town, city gates were sealed,
Until the woman bore a Son,
And prophecy fulfilled!
Bethlehem in Judea, when the censes due,
Weary travelers, by the droves,
Left your lodgings with no room.
Though little did they know it, a stable You had saved,
For worn and tired pilgrim's feet,
And a little One on the way.
Bethlehem, O Bethlehem, your name, He did make great!
For the night that He had promised came,
Revealing to the world their fate.
And a Glory once departed, made His entrance on that night,
Above the lights of Your dear city,
Angels filled the sky!
Shepherds, honored wise men, and countrymen gathered round,
They ran when they heard tidings ring,
A baby, a King, they'd found!
And although King Herod's soldiers tromped, they did not find the Son,
Though mothers lost their precious ones,
Still the enemy had not won.
O little town of Bethlehem, now about you the carolers sing,
About the night of their Savior's birth,

And the salvation He did bring!
Though small among the clans of Judah, famous you
became.
For out of you, sent from Him,
Came the Ruler, the Ancient of Days.
Over all of Israel, rests the presence of the King,
But on that night the star shone bright,
Only on Bethlehem's manger scene!

Additional Scripture references: Gen 35:19, Ruth 1:1,
1 Sam 16-17, 2 Sam 23:15-16, 1 Chron 11:16, 26,
Jer 41:16-17, Micah 5:3, Matt 2:5, Luke 2:4, 15.

Christmas

No Comparison

A voice is heard in Ramah, weeping and great mourning, Rachel weeping for her children and refusing to be comforted, because they are no more. Matthew 2:18

King Herod, furious that the Magi did not return to him with news of the whereabouts of Jesus, ordered all boys in Bethlehem two and under to be killed (2:16). How devastating! A birth that brought such joy and elation to the town of Bethlehem, would now bring agonizing death and despair. Those poor mothers and their innocent babes! Mothers whose hearts were wounded so deeply that they refused to be comforted. And all this happened because Jesus was born! What are we to think about this, Lord? The truth is, suffering and death did not cease upon Christ's birth. If anything, it increased. Yet this is exactly why He came, to bring comfort to a world filled with pain and suffering. To conquer sin and death so that we would not spend an eternity living in it. *I consider that our present sufferings are not worth comparing with the glory that will be revealed in us* (Rom 8:18). Beloved, the greater the loss, the greater the gain! A gain that cannot even be compared with the suffering we experience here on this earth. And the glory will be revealed in us, not just *to* us, but *in* us! The little life that was spared in place of all those lost would be the One to open the way for their souls to enter into eternity. He would be the only One who could bring comfort to those brokenhearted mothers who lost their baby boys. Herod, assuredly enticed by Satan, could not stop God's Divine plan to re—open the way to Himself. He could not stop Jesus from fulfilling the covenant, promised not only to the sons of Israel, but to all humanity. Even the death of so many precious babes could not compare to the glory revealed in the birth of the Son of God!

It's worth it, I say, it's worth it,
This tragedy so great!
It's worth it, I say, it's worth it,
He has thrown open the gate!

Sin may look the victor, the enemy sure to win,
But what you cannot see just yet, is the glory in the
end!

Christmas
Glory Returned

Then the glory of the LORD departed from over the threshold of the temple and stopped above the cherubim. While I watched, the cherubim spread their wings and rose from the ground, and as they went, the wheels went with them. They stopped at the entrance of the east gate of the LORD's house, and the glory of the God of Israel was above them. Ezekiel 10:18-19

The prophet Ezekiel is given an astounding vision in these passages, one which describes the glory of the Lord leaving the temple due to the wickedness and rebellion of the Israelites. Escorting the glory of the King of Kings, His messengers, the cherubim, spread their massive wings and took the Presence which had previously filled every inch of the temple back to the Heavenly throne. We know God never leaves His rightful place in the Heavenlies, but He had chosen to also dwell among His people in His earthly temple during the time of the Old Testament (1 Kings 8:1-13). Hundreds of years passed and God spoke not a word to His people through the prophets. God's people were miserable without Him. Scattered among the nations, the Israelites had been oppressed and persecuted. Those who held true to the teachings of Yahweh held out hope of His return. Faithful to His Word, the glory of the Lord came once again to dwell among His people. But this time, instead of a dark cloud and a mighty voice, our Savior came as a tender newborn babe, softly cooing at His mother's breast. The glory of the

Lord returned to the Israelites and to us! And now we see the glory, not only in a temple, but in the face of our Lord Jesus Christ. Scripture tells us of one man, a righteous man, named Simeon, who was waiting for Israel's consolation and for the coming of the Lord's Christ. As Mary and Joseph walked into the temple, they were returning the Glory to the temple! Upon His entrance, Simeon, well along in years, was finally gazing at the most beautiful child he had ever laid eyes on. A child who was to bring salvation to all people! *A light for revelation to the Gentiles and for glory to your people Israel* (Luke 2:32). Praise the Lord, Emmanuel is with us! Never to leave us, He dwells within our very being, empowering us to radiate the glory of the Lord to a world in dire need of salvation!

The Word became flesh and made his dwelling among us. We have seen His glory, the glory of the One and Only, who came from the Father, full of grace and truth. John 1:14

Christmas

Pierced Heart

And Simeon blessed them and said to Mary His mother,
'Behold, this Child is appointed for the fall and rise of many in
Israel and for a sign to be opposed—and a sword will pierce
even your own soul..." Luke 2:34-35

Oh, how could any oppose Him,
My soft, sweet baby King?
For around Him the angels have been,
And of His glory, they did sing!

Holding Him here in my arms,
With Him must I depart?
To worry if He'd come to harm,
Would break this mother's heart.

But what you prophecy here,
Simeon, all you have to say,
My heart feels joy, though does fear,
What He will face one day.

Yet all this time I've trusted,
Since the greeting from Gabriel came.
And believing the message he thus said,
Since then my life's not been the same!

Now pondering all this in my heart,
And will ponder greater still.
Since I know only in small part,
Yet beholding this baby, surreal!

When you say, "rise and fall of many,"

I think, what a perfect King!
Leading Israel onto victory,
What a wondrous sight it'd be!

Though within, my heart is troubled,
Simeon, it was something that you said.
I feel now I am humbled,
And to my Son must bow my head.

As we present our sacrifice,
Here in the temple of Yahweh,
I know these birds could never suffice,
Sin seems more than they could pay!

Could it be sweet baby has to pay it,
With His flesh and blood one day?
And on an earthly throne, never sit,
Till all that's seen has passed away?

Oh, my heart is pierced already,
But I know there's more to come!
Though by His Spirit I am steady,
I and my Savior, we are one.

Christmas
What Is Truth?

"You are a king, then!" said Pilate. Jesus answered, "You are right in saying I am a king. In fact, for this reason I was born, and for this I came into the world, to testify to the truth. Everyone on the side of truth listens to me." "What is truth?" Pilate asked. John 18:37-38

"What is truth?" Pilate asked. Jesus is truth! We live in a world that looks into the face of truth, Jesus Christ, yet does not and cannot recognize Him. Jesus came into this world to testify to Himself. Everything He said and everything He did, proclaimed Him as King over all creation. He testified to the truth of everything written about Him in Scripture. Every prophecy foretold of Him, He fulfilled. His birth, His death, and His resurrection, all point to His return and reign as our eternal King. *"You are a king, then!" said Pilate.* Yes, He is! And the reason He was born was to testify to the truth of His Sovereignty! Oh dear friend, how much of a king is Jesus to you? May we never let the truth of His Kingship fall on deaf ears, as it did Pilate's! Let us never look into the face of Jesus, yet not see Him as the King of Kings and Lord of Lords that He is! *"...for this reason I was born, and for this I came in to the world, to testify to the truth."* Why should this not be the reason for our own birth? —to continually testify to the truth that Jesus Christ is our King!

Lord, give us boldness this Christmas year,
To proclaim Your truth, and Your Name cheer!

To raise the banner in the Name of Christ,
And be witnesses of eternal life!

Christmas
Holy to the Lord

On that day HOLY TO THE LORD will be inscribed on the bells of the horses, and the cooking pots in the Lord's house will be like the sacred bowls in front of the altar. Zechariah 14:20

How sacred is Jesus to you, dear friend? When you look around your home, have you made it "holy to the Lord?" Is your home a sanctuary where the Spirit of God abides and where those who enter find peace within its walls? May there be no mistaking our sincerity and sanctity for our adorning King! In this season of pondering His infinite grace through the birth of Jesus Christ, may we never assume that all those around us have received the peace we possess. And could it be that more than the words we speak, we deliver the true message of Peace through our humble homes! With such holiday festivities among us, we must take time to not only consecrate our hearts, but also our habitats. May we remove that which might hinder the gentle workings of the Holy Spirit in the lives of those whose hearts have become hardened or even broken. Let us entertain this Christmas season in homes that clearly portray the reason for the season. And let us make sacred that which brings us together and see everything we do and possess as an avenue for Divine grace to be imparted!

Purify our hearts, Lord,
Purify our homes.
Make them holy unto You,

Make them now Your own.

Sanctify the season,
Consecrate the time,
Be the only reason,
Be the One we magnify.

Lead those to salvation,
Who fellowship therein,
May their souls foresee elation,
When their lives, You enter in!

New Years

Crown the Year

You crown the year with Your bounty, and Your carts overflow with abundance. Blessed are those You choose and bring near to live in Your courts! We are filled with the good things of Your house, of Your holy temple. Psalms 65:11, 4

There is a freshness and newness which accompanies the beginning year. All of January seems to offer us a chance to start anew on long awaited interests or give us the boldness to end that which may have only proved to weigh us down in the year past. But more than its offer of second chances, a new year brings with it new mercies. Satan wants nothing more than for us to only dwell on the hardships we faced in this past year. Yet, if we see each trial and each triumph as coming from the hand of a loving God who can use even our most overwhelming temptations to shape our character into His likeness, then we will understand that the Lord surely dealt bountifully with us! We will understand that each year of our lives has been crowned with His goodness and that our treasure can never be measured by the world's standards. If God has chosen to bring us near to live in His courts, then there will be no end to the abundance of grace which Christ so freely and generously extends! We may not have been filled with good things by the measure of our circumstances last year, but we can be sure we have been filled with the good things from the House of the Lord. For within His holy temple there is righteousness, peace, hope, steadfast assurance, quietness, and rest. There is mercy and grace poured forth from our great High Priest who still lives to daily intercede for us! So as we begin this year, let us seek the bounty of Christ, yearning for everything we have been promised by Him who infuses the power of the Godhead into our lives through the blessed Holy Spirit!

Crown us with Your bounty, Lord,
As this new year comes our way!
Bless us now, Lord, more and more,
With an abundance of Your grace!
You did not withhold Your mercies,
As we ponder last year's fate,
And now, Lord, make us thirsty,
For Your righteousness awaits!
Blessed we are and chosen,
By Your providential hand.
Precious covenant unbroken,
Rescued from sin's desert land.
So fill us with Your goodness,
Let us worship in Your courts!
For within Your Holy Temple
You're our unlimited resource!

New Years

A New Year's Promise

Rest in God alone, my soul, for my hope comes from Him.
Psalm 62:5, HCSB

Oh Lord, what will this New Year bring,
What paths will we venture, sight unseen?
Trial, heartache, sadness, stress?
Peace, comfort, quiet rest.
Tragedy, injury, loss, death?
Peace, comfort, quiet rest.
Disappointment, depression, failure, regress?
Peace, comfort, quiet rest.
Joyful, happy, content, blest?
Peace, comfort, quiet rest.
Increase, abundance, promotion, success?
Peace, comfort, quiet rest.
Oh Lord, what will this New Year bring,
What paths we'll venture, sight unseen?
We know not what this New Year brings,
Nor the results of the future things.
But whatever it brings, the worst or the best,
You'll give us Your peace, Your comfort, Your rest.

New Years

A New Year's Therapy

Therefore, strengthen your feeble arms and weak knees.
Hebrews 12:12

Though we are encouraged not to dwell in the past, we are, on the other hand, incited to learn from it. Therefore, when recounting the previous year, let us carefully consider the need to mend our "feeble arms" or "weak knees." We can accomplish this by examining the preceding year's opportunities that were not fully embraced due to the shallowness of our faith or the overwhelming difficulty of our circumstances. We can examine all the vain attempts made on our behalf, which we boosted with the giddy presumption of God's approval. We can take inventory of the times when we sacrificed our gaining spiritual depth and maturity during those privileged, quiet moments of our day in order to merely entertain our flesh with less worthy accommodations. Nevertheless, today, the first and most refreshing days of a new year, may we not give way to our past defeat, but rather directly apply spiritual therapy to strengthen the very weaknesses we recall! Let us do so by simplifying the material entanglements, which negate the clarity of our minds, satisfying our soul's longings with spiritual necessities, and sanctifying that which has been spoiled by worldly influences. Most importantly, let us signify our Master by living with a new measure of integrity before all who we encounter. As we turn another page of life's fleeting years, may we strive, being strengthened in character and sound judgment, to make profitable investments not in our own affairs, but rather, the Kingdom's!

Lord, apply Your healing balm,
To my weakened knee!
And strengthen now this feeble arm,
All tightened joints, please free!

Eager to start the coming year,
Lord, what can I improve?
Recall when faith gave way to fear,
Or if I stalled when You said move?

Did I waste the time allotted me?
Did I coddle daily stress?
Did I struggle in the monotony,
Instead of giving each day my best?

Many mistakes against me testify,
Even those I faint recall.
And a one I couldn't er' deny,
Even if some of them seem small.

Though I have a blessed Healer,
Who provides me therapy!
And as we work, He draws me nearer,
To strengthen my heart and whole body!

And with the breath of a crisp year unfolding,
My New Year's remedy, You have assigned.
Make my efforts in full, none withholding,
Your Spirit with my limbs entwine!

New Years

A New Year's Blessing

You will still be eating last year's harvest when you will have to move it out to make room for the new. Leviticus 26:10

What a glorious reminder this New Year of God's unfailing love and faithfulness to us! His supply of spiritual blessing never runs dry! Now He brings us to the start of a new year of overflowing abundance; a place where we must distribute the excess of all that He has supplied us with, in order to receive more. Yet even in our apportioning, we never lose any of the nourishment and growth we received from the last year's harvest. So how are we to make room for more spiritual blessing? Where do we take last year's harvest and with whom do we share it? The answer...we give from the overflow of our storehouses of faith! We take what we have reaped back into the fields. We take it to those whose year was struck with famine and are still experiencing severe drought. They now need the same spiritual nourishment we have already received. Who do you know that is in need of being nurtured back to spiritual health in the coming year? May we take our harvest of spiritual blessings to those impoverished and continue ourselves feasting on the promised bounty of the New Year!

The toil and strife of last year's reap,
Have only served to nourish me!
Just when we thought we had run dry,
Your Spirit poured forth rich blessings nigh!

But where now do we store all this?
Your mercy and grace, we dare not miss!
Then the Lord of the Harvest stooped down to say,
"Look to the fields, they are wasting away,
The drought and famine led many astray.
So fill your sacks and take the grain,
Spread it around, I'll send the rain.
Then open wide your storehouse doors,
And I'll fill this year with even more!"

72993626R00189

Made in the USA
Lexington, KY
06 December 2017